The Complete
PalmPilot Guide

The Complete PalmPilot Guide

Calvin O. Parker

A Division of Henry Holt
and Company, Inc.

MIS :Press
A Division of Henry Holt and Company, Inc.
115 West 18th Street
New York, New York 10011
http://www.mispress.com

Copyright © 1998 by M&T Books

Printed in the United States of America

First Edition—1998

ISBN: 1-55828-586-5

MIS:Press and M&T Books are available at special discounts for bulk purchases for sales promotions, premiums, and fundraising.

For details contact: Special Sales Director
                          MIS:Press and M&T Books
                          Divisions of Henry Holt and Company, Inc.
                          115 West 18th Street
                          New York, New York 10011

10 9 8 7 6 5 4 3

Associate Publisher: *Paul Farrell*

Managing Editor: *Shari Chappell*	**Copy Edit Manager:** *Karen Tongish*
Editor: *Rebekah Young*	**Copy Editor:** *Janice Borzendowski*
Production Editor: *Danielle DeLucia*	**Technical Editor:** *John J. Lehett*

Acknowledgments

I'd like to start out by thanking my loving wife, Ginny. She was six months pregnant when I began working on this book, and it wasn't easy to commit to a project that would take so much of my time. Fortunately, she agreed with me that this type of opportunity doesn't come along very often and that I should do it. Somehow, I've managed to write a book and juggle all the other things in my life during these last few months, due in no small part to the help of this wonderful lady. Thank you, Ginny.

I'd also like to thank my son Trevor, who did a pretty good job of understanding that Daddy needed to be left alone to work—no small feat for a three-year-old. Thanks also go to our newest addition, Jordan, who is still trying hard to figure this whole human being thing out.

Next in line is Christopher Olson, who wrote the chapter on programming. Chris is probably one of the sharpest folks working with me here, and he has been involved with technical writing for years. When I told him I needed someone to help me with the programming chapter, he jumped at the opportunity. Chris produced a chapter I'd have been hard-pressed to match on my own. Thanks again, Chris.

I'd also like to thank John Lehett, the technical editor for this project. John brought his experience with the PalmPilot to bear and always managed to provide comments and suggestions within a couple of days of receiving each piece of the manuscript. John's been a good resource, and he's been a good friend.

I'd also like to thank Edward Keyes, of Daggerware fame. When I had difficulty creating the Macintosh side of the CD-ROM that accompanies this book, Ed went out of his way to help out. Ed has also been instrumental throughout the book whenever I had a Mac question and has attended almost every single IRC night to answer the impromptu questions I've had. Thanks Ed.

Special thanks also go to the handful of folks who have helped me with the book project and FAQ site. In no particular order, I'd like to thank Donald Parker, Bill Kirby, Rick Bram, Jeff Jetton, Kenny West, Kevin McCabe, Rick Huebner, Alan Weiner, Chris "Sparky" Burnett, James Iuliano, Nick Bradbury, Yanek Martinson, Mark Pierce, Tracy Reed, the folks from #pilot-pda, the folks at MIS:Press, and everyone who contributed to the PalmPilot mailing list and newsgroups. I couldn't have done it without you.

Finally, I'd like to thank all of the PalmPilot developers out there, particularly those who allowed us to include their applications on the book's CD-ROM. Thanks, folks—keep those wonderful applications coming!

Introduction

In the spring of 1996, I read an article about a new product from U.S. Robotics called the Pilot. Right away, I knew I wanted one. Scouring the Internet, I tried to determine if the device was as cool as it sounded. Satisfied that it was, I ordered a Pilot 1000 in late August. Within days of purchasing it and installing what few applications there were available at the time, I ordered the 1MB upgrade, thinking that 1MB of memory would be sufficient.

In early November, I started compiling material for a Frequently Asked Questions (FAQ) list. When another FAQ appeared on the scene, I put my project aside for awhile but picked it back up again when it became apparent that the FAQ wasn't going to be as comprehensive or as frequently updated as I felt it should be. My FAQ site went up in January 1997. I immediately started asking folks to place links to my site on their sites. My first big break came when Adam Deaves, who maintained what was then the most popular PalmPilot software site, placed a prominent link at the top of his main page.

A lot has happened since then. I've passed my original Pilot 1000 along to a friend and replaced it with a PalmPilot Professional (with 2MB of memory!). I've also managed to impress enough folks with the site to warrant a link on most PalmPilot Web sites. I've moved the FAQ site to a separate Web host service, due to heavy traffic. The pages now garner upward of 8000 hits a day, and I receive e-mail from all corners of the globe.

What started out as a quick letter from the publisher about the possibility of writing a book has grown into the book you know hold in your hands. *The Complete PalmPilot Guide* is the culmination of several months' work. I hope it will help just as many (if not more) folks as my FAQ site does. Although a good bit of the book's content is derived from the Web pages, I've tried to supplement and update it so that even folks with Internet access will feel as if they've gotten something out of the book that the site doesn't provide. Starting with a simple description of the PalmPilot, this book will present little-known tips and tricks, discuss available software, and briefly hit on the programming possibilities and potential of the PalmPilot.

In writing this book, my goal was to reveal the wonderful world of the PalmPilot to those who might not have an Internet connection or who might not have discovered any of the fabulous Web sites now dedicated to it. I think that I've managed to do just that, and I hope that you'll feel the same way.

CONTENTS

CHAPTER 1

INTRODUCING THE PALMPILOT

In This Chapter

- What is the PalmPilot?
- What comes with the PalmPilot
- Shortcomings of the original Pilot
- New PalmPilot models
- Platforms supported

What Is the Pilot?

The PalmPilot is a hand-held personal organizer and palmtop computer made by U.S. Robotics' (now 3Com) Palm Computing Division. Since its release in the second quarter of 1996, the PalmPilot has become the most popular hand-held organizer on the market, reportedly selling at a rate of 1 out of every 4 electronic organizers. At 3 by 4-3/4 by 5/8 inches, this tiny device, powered by two AAA batteries that last several weeks on average, outperforms most of its competitors and compares favorably to organizers and PDAs that cost twice as much.

NOTE

Due to a dispute over the name "Pilot, " 3Com now refers to the device as the PalmPilot, and asks that others do the same in both printed and electronic materials. Therefore, every attempt has been made to do so in this book. Also, most of the references in this book are to version 2.0 of PalmOS. Although I try to point out when version 2.0 differs from the older version, if you see something that doesn't sound familiar, and I don't address it, it's probably because you're using version 1.0.

The PalmPilot comes standard with a carrying case (a vinyl slipcover), HotSync cradle, the Desktop software, and some documentation. In short, you get everything you need to connect and synchronize the PalmPilot with your desktop computer—aside from this book.

Nothing's Perfect

The first version of any product usually has a few problems, and the PalmPilot is no exception. When the first version came out, most owners probably would have agreed that the case could have been sturdier, the stylus slot was too easy to crack, the screen was too easy to scratch, and so on. The product has since been modified to fix these problems, and any others were eclipsed by the PalmPilot's benefits. Most evident of these are the operating system, PalmOS, and the sheer ease with which data and programs can be transferred to and from the PalmPilot. It is this user friend-liness, coupled with the low price point, that has made the PalmPilot so popular.

A New Era

The new PalmPilot models (released in March 1997) added a few hardware modifications (of which backlighting is the most significant), several new OS enhancements, and an expense tracker and e-mail support.

NOTE

The Expense and E-mail applications are built in to the Professional PalmPilot model. The Expense application can be installed on the Personal model, but the E-mail application is available only on the Professional model.

Although owners of old versions of the PalmPilot can't upgrade to the new backlit display without purchasing a new machine, 3Com offered generous rebates for several months following the new model's release. 3Com also released a 1MB version 2.0 OS upgrade board. This upgrade board enables owners of older Pilots to run version 2.0 of the PalmPilotOS and adds TCP/IP support (the board can also be installed in the PalmPilot Personal to upgrade it to the Professional models).

Figure 1.1 Start-up screens fo PalmOS 1.0 (left) and 2.0 (right).

For more information on the difference between versions 1.0 and 2.0 of PalmOS, see Chapter 2, PalmPilot Basics.

ROADMAP

Multiplatform Support

Currently supported OS platforms include:

- Windows (3.1, 95, Windows for Workgroups, and NT)
- Macintosh
- OS/2 Warp (WIN-OS/2 sessions)
- UNIX/Linux

Support for the PalmPilot focuses primarily on Windows 95. Although it is possible to synchronize your data on all four platforms, full support, including third-party conduits, is mainly for Windows 95.

NOTE

Conclusion

Now that you know what a PalmPilot is, let's take a look at some of the basic features, applications, and capabilities of the device in the next chapter, "PalmPilot Basics."

CHAPTER 2

PalmPilot Basics

In This Chapter

- Comparing the old and new PalmPilot models
- Software changes from PalmOS 1.0 to PalmOS 2.0
- PalmPilot's built-in applications
- PalmPilot Desktop
- The operating system: PalmOS
- Adding applications to your PalmPilot
- 3Com's service/repair policy
- PalmPilot accessories

The documentation that accompanies all PalmPilots includes much useful information. This chapter will only briefly cover this information, instead concentrating on various tips and hints that the documentation doesn't emphasize.

Comparing the Old and New PalmPilot Models

There are two different aspects to the PalmPilot: the unit itself and the memory/ROM board. The various model designations (Pilot 1000, Pilot 5000, PalmPilot Personal, and PalmPilot Professional) indicate the type of memory/ROM board the unit contains.

Old vs. New

The older PalmPilot's deficiencies include no backlighting and the plastic is not as sturdy as that of the newer PalmPilot boxes. (Remember, this is true for the older versions of the original PalmPilot only. The later versions of the older models have better screen contrast, scratch resistance, etc.) The name difference is readily apparent: above the screen it reads "Pilot," as opposed to "PalmPilot." In some older PalmPilot machines, a screw behind the screen causes problems. Another screw is hidden beneath the sticker on the back of the unit, rendering it invisible; consequently, the case could not be taken apart easily. Other than those elements and the model number, 1000/5000, there is no difference between the 1000 and the 5000 models (and the board section, as explained next).

As you already know, the PalmPilot is backlit, the plastic case is sturdier, and the troublesome screw on some older units has been moved or eliminated. There is now an opening in the sticker that enables access to the third screw. The upgrade board is the only significant difference between the Personal and the Professional versions (see The ROM/Memory Board section, next).

3Com recognized the significance of third-party applications and their impact on memory requirements. The first wave of PalmPilots had 128K and 512K of RAM respectively; the newer PalmPilots have a base of 512K and 1024K of available RAM.

The ROM/Memory Board

The memory board comes in five different versions, but *any* board will fit in *any* Pilot, making replacements across models possible.

- 128K memory/1.0 OS: The version in the PalmPilot 1000.

- 512K memory/1.0 OS: The version in the PalmPilot 5000.

- 1MB memory/1.0 OS: The older "upgrade" board. Used to upgrade the older PalmPilots to 1MB.

- 512K memory/2.0 OS without TCP/IP: The version in the PalmPilot Personal.

- 1MB memory/2.0 OS with TCP/IP: The version in the PalmPilot Professional. This is also the board contained in the 1MB PalmPilot Professional upgrade.

The memory board also contains the Expense application and the E-mail application in ROM. The 1.0 OS is contained in a 512K ROM; the 2.0 OS uses a 1MB ROM. This is not the same as the RAM just outlined. The preceding configurations are the "off-the-shelf" memory configurations. Since the release of the newer PalmPilot models, several companies have been offering to upgrade the standard memory configurations to 2, or even 3 megabytes! See Chapter 4, Troubleshooting the PalmPilot: Common Q&A, for more information about how these boards can be upgraded.

Figure 2.1 The Memory screen, showing the amount of free memory on a new PalmPilot Professional.

New Model, New OS

Along with adding backlighting to the new PalmPilots comes operating system upgrades. Specifically, OS 2.0 is the version on the 512K PalmPilot Personal, and OS 2.0 Pro is the version on the 1MB PalmPilot Professional. OS 2.0 Pro is identical to OS 2.0 except for the addition of TCP/IP capability and the E-mail application. Also, the Expense and E-mail applications are contained in ROM on the 2.0 Pro OS boards. The major difference is in the software, which includes a rumored 250-plus enhancements and changes. Following is a list of the most important changes:

- The Preferences app now appears in the last "mode" you accessed. These modes are:
  - Buttons, which allows you to define an app to run from the hardware buttons, and the calculator silkscreen button.
  - Digitizer, which is the same as before, but the crosshairs look nicer.
  - Formats, which have added presets for several countries.

- General, which now has Alarm Sound and Game Sound check-boxes added to the System Sound checkbox.

- Modem, which may be accessed here or from the HotSync app.

- Network (2.0 Pro only) is where you set up service, User Name/Password, and Phone number information for network access. It also defines TCP/IP connection type, time-out, primary/secondary DNS, and how the IP address is determined.

- Owner is a MemoPad-like screen for entering whatever you like. It launches with "This PalmPilot is owned by:" but this can be deleted or changed. Information entered here is displayed at powerup after locking the device via the Lock and Off feature in the Security app.

- You can now tap corners of the graffiti area (site of letters and numbers) to bring up the keyboard or number pad.

- A new month view has been added (Figure 2.2).

Figure 2.2 The new PalmOS 2.0 Month view.

- An improved Week view displays appointments as "bars" and allows you to drag appointments; tapping on the bar will result in a pop-up displaying the details of that appointment.

- New scroll bars have been added to memos.

- A Lookup function enables you to insert names and phone numbers from Phone Book.
- You can now highlight text and then press the **Find** button to place that text in the Find window.
- You can tap found items; this takes you there without additional press (and without waiting for the screen to fill).
- Tap the date at the top of the window in DateBook to show time.
- You can now define nonaudible alarms for untimed events.
- A new Preferences option shows only used lines in DateBook.
- Remember Last Category functionality has been added to DateBook preferences.
- Different sorting options are offered for to-do's.
- The MemoPad app now allows alphabetic or manual sorting.
- Each memo in MemoPad is now numbered.
- The Turn off and lock capability is now available as a keystroke (defined in preferences).
- Giraffe game is now available in ROM.
- Graffiti help is accessible from all apps.
- An alarm indicator is included on DateBook entries.
- DateBook has day/week/month view icons.
- The Graffiti stroke that brought up the keyboard is now customizable (turn on/off backlight, keyboard, Graffiti help, off, and lock).
- Alarms for timed events sound every five minutes until acknowledged.
- Auto Capitalization has been improved.
- The Memory app now displays applications in alphabetical order (and in the Delete screen).

- The Delete app screen now scrolls using the hardware buttons.
- In ToDo prefs, you can specify to record the completion date when an item is checked.
- In the ToDo app, you can now show Categories (when **All** is selected).

Built-In Applications

A major attraction of the PalmPilot is its suite of four built-in applications—DateBook, AddressBook, ToDo List, and MemoPad. Of course, it is impossible to please all the users all the time, but the PalmPilot's built-in applications manage to cover most of the bases. First we'll look at some common elements of these applications, then cover each in more detail.

Common Elements

Although each built-in application serves a different purpose, all of them have some features in common. These include:

- The AddressBook, ToDo List, and MemoPad applications allow you to group your records in user-defined categories.
- Each application allows editing of key record details through the **Details** button/command.
- The DateBook, AddressBook, and ToDo List applications allow you to attach a note to each record.
- The DateBook, ToDo List, and MemoPad applications allow you to perform a phone number lookup out of the AddressBook application.
- All four applications can be invoked either by pressing the hardware button associated with that application, or by selecting it in the application picker.

- All four applications' records can be marked as private.
- All four applications allow adding a new entry via the **New** button.

Categories

Most PalmPilot applications let you specify a category for each item of an application, so that you can group like records together. For example, you can keep all of your personal contacts in the Personal category of the AddressBook application, and all of your business contacts in the Business category. And most applications that support categories allow you to change a record category in that record's Details window.

To add, rename, or delete categories, select **Edit Categories** from any drop-down menu where you would normally set the category.

Hardware Buttons

By default, each of the four main built-in applications is associated with one of the hardware buttons, which from left to right are: DateBook, AddressBook, ToDo List, and MemoPad (see Figure 2.3). (Note, though, that an application run by a given button may be set. See the section on system preferences later in this chapter.) The applications subsequently can be easily accessed by selecting these buttons.

Figure 2.3 The Hardware buttons.

Details

For each record, you may set certain aspects, attach a note, or delete the record via the Details window. This window, accessible through the **Details** button, contains specific items for each of the built-in applications as described in the following subsections.

Notes

The DateBook, AddressBook, and ToDo List applications allow you to attach a note to each record. Select the **Note** button in the Details window to bring up the Edit Note screen. Notes appear as little note icons for records that contain one; the note can be edited by tapping on that icon. Text in attached notes is also searched when you use the **Find** feature, allowing you to place keywords or other important terms in the record.

Phone Lookup

In three of the built-in applications (the AddressBook is the exception) you can insert an AddressBook entry's name and phone number into the current item or record. To do this, use the **Phone Lookup** command from the Options menu; or use the **Graffiti** command stroke and an **L** to bring up the Phone Number Lookup screen, which is essentially the AddressBook screen with **Add** and **Cancel** buttons. Scroll or perform a lookup by writing the first few characters of a name; select an entry, then press the **Add** button. This will insert the name (both first and last), along with the phone field specified in the Show in List option of that record, into the item currently being edited.

Private Records

To mark a record as private, set the Security option to **Hide Private Records** in the Details window. Doing so enables you to hide sensitive information from view. The Security application and private records are covered later in this chapter.

Throughout all the built-in applications, you can delete any text by highlighting it and using the backspace Graffiti character.

TIP

That's it for the common elements. We'll now address the applications themselves.

DateBook

The DateBook application is where you enter and track your appointments and schedule. With this application you can:

- *Track important (and not so important) dates and events.* These events may be either timed or untimed. For example, a birthday or anniversary wouldn't have a time associated with it, whereas an important meeting would.

- *Schedule events to repeat.* This allows you to define an event as one that takes place on a regular basis, so that you don't have to enter the information more than once. Examples of this are birthdays and weekly staff meetings.

- *Set alarms to remind you of events.* Alarms can be set to sound at a specific time per event. You can set an alarm to ring 10 minutes before that meeting down the hall, and half an hour before you have to pick up the kids at school.

- *Attach notes to each event.* The optional note feature, available in all of the built-in applications (except for MemoPad), allows you to attach a descriptive note to each event.

- *View your daily schedule, including overlapping appointments.* The Daily view displays all of your upcoming appointments, including their scheduled times (using the View Time Bars preference).

- *View your weekly schedule.* The Weekly view displays a barchart view of your week's events, including conflicts. One tap on a bar quickly displays the important information for that appointment, eliminating the need to switch between day and weekly views.

- *View your monthly schedule.* The monthly view allows you, at a glance, to see on which days of the month you have appointments and on which ones you are free.

Getting Started

To activate the DateBook application, press the **DateBook** button or tap the **DateBook** icon in the application picker. The first time you run the application, you will see a blank Daily view (Figure 2.4).

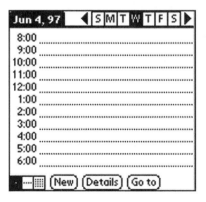

Figure 2.4 An empty DateBook Daily view.

Adding Events

There are several ways to add an event to the DateBook:

- *Tap on a displayed time in the Daily view.* This will bring up the Set Time window, where you can specify the time(s) for the event. From this window, click the **OK** button to return to the Daily view with the cursor on the line ready to input the name or description of the event.

- *Tap on a line next to the time and start writing.* This will add an event for that time.

ROADMAP

Entering text using Graffiti is covered later in this chapter.

- *Start writing without selecting anything.* If you start writing a letter, that text will show up as the text for an untimed event. If you start writing a number, you will be presented with the Set Time window, with that number used as the start time for the event.

- *Tap the **New** button.* This brings up a blank Set Time window to specify the start and end times for an event.

TIP

To specify an untimed event when presented with the Set Time window, tap on the **No Time** button.

Purging Events

To save space in the PalmPilot, you can purge items that are older than a predetermined amount of time by using the **Purge** option of the Record menu. This brings up the Purge window, where you can choose 1 week, 2 weeks, 3 weeks, or 1 month. You also have the option to save deleted events in an archive copy on your PC.

NOTE Whenever you delete an item from PalmPilot, you are given the option to save it in an archive copy on your PC. This builds a file on your PC that you can later restore using the Desktop. The section on the PalmPilot Desktop has more information on restoring data from archive copies.

Available Views

The DateBook application offers three views of your schedule. To switch between these three views, use the **View Selection** button in the lower left of the screen. The Day view is the default when the application is first run, and this is highlighted. The second button represents the weekly view, the third button the monthly view. Figure 2.5 show the Weekly and Monthly views, with the appropriate button selection highlighted.

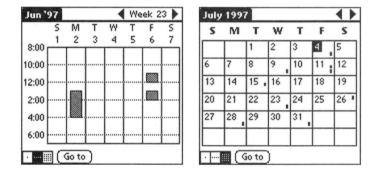

Figure 2.5 The DateBook's Weekly (left) and Monthly (right) views.

You can also use the various views to jump to a specific day, week, or month. Simply press the **Go to** button, located in all three views, and you are presented with a slight variation on the Monthly view, from which you can jump quickly to any year, month, week, or day (view-dependent).

TIP

Use the **Page Up** and **Page Down** keys to move forward or backward one increment in whichever view you are located. For example, if you are in the month view, and would like to quickly jump forward a month, press the **Page Down** key. This capability often makes it easier to switch to a particular view as opposed to going through the **Go to** button.

Details

For each event, you can set an alarm, define the event as repeating, attach a note, and mark the event as private. To set these options, place the cursor in the event and press the **Details** button.

ROADMAP

The Private flag is discussed later in this chapter in the section on the Security application.

TIP

You can direct all events to automatically use a preset alarm by accessing the alarm preset in the DateBook Preferences window.

To define an event as repeating, press the word **None** on the Repeat line to access the Change Repeat window. This feature is very flexible, enabling you to specify repeat events by day, week, month, or year, and monthly repeating events as a date or day (such as the second Tuesday of each month). The weekly repeat lets you specify multiple events for each week, such as an event that repeats every week on Monday, Tuesday, and Friday. See Figure 2.6 for an example of the Weekly view of the Change Repeat window.

Figure 2.6 The Weekly view of the Change Repeat window.

DateBook Preferences

Several options and preferences are available for the DateBook application under the Options menu. You can determine:

- The start and end times to display in the Day view (Preferences).

To display only time lines for those that have events on them, set the start and end time the same; for example, 7:00 A.M.

- Whether to set an alarm automatically, and for what time period (Preferences).
- Whether to display the Time Bars and a compressed Day view (Display Options).
- Which events to display (Timed, Untimed, Repeating) in the Month view (Display Options).

AddressBook

The AddressBook application is where you keep track of your contacts, whether personal or professional. With this application you can:

- Add, edit, and delete information about friends, companies, and other contacts.
- Sort contacts by category and either last name or company name.
- Quickly locate a contact by using the **Lookup** feature.
- Rename and utilize up to four different custom field names.

Getting Started

To activate the AddressBook application, press the **AddressBook** button or tap the **AddressBook** icon in the application picker. The first time you run the application, you will see the Address List in the All category, with the standard Palm Computing entries already added (Figure 2.7).

Figure 2.7 The initial AddressBook screen.

Adding a Contact

To add a new contact, tap on the **New** button. You will be placed in the Address Edit window, with the cursor in the top field, Last Name. At this point, you can begin to add the information to each field. The fields with the drop-down menu indicator (a small downward arrow) indicate the fields that can be changed. This allows you to list a contact with multiple e-mail addresses or more than one business phone, for example.

If you are entering information using Graffiti, you can move from field to field with the **Next Field** (straight down and up stroke) and **Previous Field** (straight up and down stroke) Graffiti strokes.

Note that the last four fields are called Custom 1, Custom 2, Custom 3, and Custom 4. We will cover how to change these in just a moment.

Finding a Contact: Lookup

To locate an entry in a long list of contacts (for example, if you have the **All** category selected), use the **Lookup** feature. Simply start writing in Graffiti; the entry that begins with the letter or letters you write will be displayed.

Details

For each contact, in the Show in List item, you can specify in which category the contact should be placed and whether to mark the record as private. To set these options, tap the **Details** button in the Address Edit screen.

The Show in List item in the Details window determines which of the phone numbers in the record will display first in the Address List when the AddressBook application is run. This number is also pasted with the name when the entry is selected via the **Phone Lookup** feature.

Preferences

The AddressBook Preferences window, shown in Figure 2.8, is available only from the Address List Options menu. This screen is where you can specify whether you want the last category accessed to display or that you'd prefer to list addresses by last name, first name or company name, last name. If you choose not to display the last category accessed, each invocation of the AddressBook application will start in the All category, displaying all records.

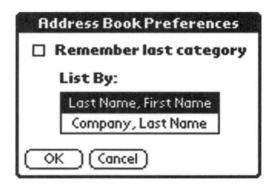

Figure 2.8 The AddressBook Preferences window.

Also available from the Options menu is the **Rename Custom Fields** option. This enables you to change the name of the four custom fields to whatever you'd like.

NOTE

There are only four custom fields, so use them wisely. Some of the more common uses for these fields are Birthdate, Account #, Misc., and so on. Be aware that changing the custom field names will trigger an informational message in the HotSync log about that field name change the next time you HotSync.

ToDo List

The ToDo List application is the PalmPilot's checklist. With this application you can:

- Add items that need to be addressed, including a due date and priority.
- Sort ToDo items by priority and due date, due date and priority, category and priority, or category and due date.
- Record completion dates for handled items.

Getting Started

To activate the ToDo List application, press the **ToDo List** button or tap the **ToDo List** icon in the application picker. The first time you run the application, you will see the ToDo List in the All category, with the standard Palm Computing entries added (Figure 2.9).

Figure 2.9 Initial ToDo List screen.

Adding ToDo Items

To add a ToDo item, tap the **New** button. The ToDo List application is unique in that the individual records are not entered and edited on their own screens, but on the main one, the ToDo List screen. Therefore, adding a new item simply results in a blank ToDo item, as shown in Figure 2.10.

Figure 2.10 Adding a new ToDo item.

Each ToDo List item has four parts: Priority, Item text, Due Date, and Category. When you tap on the **New** button, the new item added is automatically given a priority of 1, no due date, and the same category as the currently viewed item (or Unfiled, if you are in the All or Unfiled categories).

TIP

If you tap in an existing item and then on the **New** button, the new entry will be added with the same priority, due date, and category as the entry selected.

Preferences: What to Show

By default, only the priority of each item is displayed, but you can change this by tapping the **Show** button. This brings up the ToDo Preferences screen, shown in Figure 2.11. Here you specify the items to sort by, and which items you'd like displayed in the main ToDo List screen. You can also specify whether to record completion dates for those items you check off.

Figure 2.11 The ToDo Preferences screen.

Removing Completed Items

ToDo List items checked as completed are not automatically removed. You have to manually remove them. To do this, use the **Purge** selection on the Record menu. This will bring up the Purge window, which confirms that you want to delete all ToDo items that have been marked as completed, and asks if you want to save an archive copy on your PC.

NOTE

If you don't have **Show Completed Items** selected in the ToDo Preferences, it may *seem* like the items are deleted when you check them off, but they are not. If you find your ToDo List application running slower and slower, this might be the reason. Remember to run the **Purge** option periodically to empty completed items.

MemoPad

The MemoPad application is the memo and notes application for the PalmPilot. Memos are identical to the notes you're familiar with in the other applications, except that they aren't tied to any other record. With the MemoPad application you can:

- Compose memos and arrange them by category.
- Sort your list of memos automatically or manually.

Getting Started

To activate the MemoPad application, press the **MemoPad** button or tap the **MemoPad** icon in the application picker. The first time you run the application, you will see the Memo List in the All category, with the standard Palm Computing entries added (see Figure 2.12).

Figure 2.12 The initial MemoPad List screen.

Adding a Memo

To add a memo, tap the **New** button in the Memo List screen. You will be presented with a blank memo. Alternatively, you can just start writing using either Graffiti or the keyboard, and you will automatically begin composing a new memo.

The first line of a memo is displayed in the Memo List screen and in the Memo List window of the Desktop software, in alphabetical order (by default). If you choose to have memos sort automatically, you can determine the order in which they will appear by naming them appropriately.

Details

While in a memo, tap the **Details** button to access the Memo Details window. Here you can set the category for the memo, as well as mark it as private.

Preferences

The Memo Preferences window, invoked by the **Preferences** item in the Options menu, allows you to decide whether to sort your memos alphabetically or manually.

To sort your memos manually, simply drag and drop each memo where you'd like it to reside in the Memo List.

What's Left

Eight other applications come built into the PalmPilot: Calc, Expense (Professional model only), Giraffe, HotSync, Mail (Professional model only), Memory, Prefs, and Security. With the exception of the Mail application, these applications are covered in the PalmPilot documentation, so the following subsections cover each application only briefly.

The Expense and Mail applications were added with the 2.0 version of PalmOS, and are available to owners of the older PalmPilot models only if they upgrade to PalmOS 2.0.

ROADMAP

The Mail application is discussed in more detail in Chapter 3, Portability and Connectivity.

Calc

Calc is the built-in calculator application. It's nothing fancy, just a simple calculator. (For those looking for more, there are several shareware and commercial calculators available.) By default, you launch this application by tapping on the **Calculator** silkscreen button.

Expense

This simple application enables you to keep a log of expenses, and saves its information on the PC each HotSync session. This information is subsequently passed over to a desktop spreadsheet application when you press the **Expense** button on the PalmPilot Desktop.

Giraffe

In this game of falling letters, you can practice your Graffiti skills.

HotSync

HotSync runs on the PalmPilot and the Desktop when you synchronize data. To start it, press the button on the cradle. For more information on the HotSync process, see Chapter 3, Portability and Connectivity.

Mail

The Mail application is unique in that it doesn't sync any data with the Pilot Desktop application. Instead, it requires the use of a supported third-party mail application. When properly configured, the Mail application will sync the mail with the desktop program, marking mail that is read and deleting mail that has been deleted on your desktop PC.

Memory

The Memory function is used to display which applications you have installed on your PalmPilot, how much total memory you have, and how much memory is currently being used. Memory is also used to delete any applications that you have installed, via the **Delete Apps** button.

Prefs

The Prefs application is where all of the PalmPilot's system preferences are set. The various Preferences screens are available from the upper-right corner's menu (similar to the normal category pull-down). These screens are:

- *Buttons*. Used to define which applications are run when one of the four hardware buttons or calculator silkscreen button is pressed. Also defines which application to run when the cradle and modem buttons are pressed, and what action to take when the Graffiti upstroke (used by default to bring up the keyboard) is used.

- *Digitizer*. Used to calibrate the touch-screen's digitizer. Runs when the unit is initially powered up; then only needs to be run if you notice the touch-screen is not recognizing your screen presses accurately.

- *Formats*. Allows you to set options such as Date, Time, and Number formats, and the day on which to start. Includes presets for 24 countries.

- *General*. Allows you to set the time and date, the auto-off time, and the state of the various system sounds.

- *Modem*. Used to specify settings for the modem.

- *Owner*. Lets you enter the text that is displayed on the screen when the unit is powered back on after you turn it off with the **Off and Lock** function (available in the Security application, described next).

- *Shortcuts.* By adding, deleting, and editing system shortcuts, you can enter text using the shortcut Graffiti stroke, then the name of the shortcut. For example, the shortcut **br** is installed by default, and would be replaced by the word Breakfast (see Figure 2.13).

Figure 2.13 The Shortcuts Preferences screen, showing the default shortcuts.

Security

In the Security application, the PalmPilot password is set and changed. You can also use the Security application's Turn Off & Lock Device feature to turn off and lock the PalmPilot. This will display the Owner screen (specified in the Owner screen of Prefs) and require the password to be entered the next time the PalmPilot is turned on. This is also the application where you turn on and off the display of records that are marked as private.

NOTE

The capability to turn off and lock the PalmPilot is available to software developers, and has been used in several shareware and freeware applications. Perhaps the most popular of these is Check-In, by Jack Russell. This application not only can turn off and lock the PalmPilot, it also can be configured to automatically lock the PalmPilot and/or hide all private records every time the PalmPilot is turned off and back on. See Chapter 6, PalmPilot Shareware, for more information.

NOTE

The Private flag is one that can be set on every record in the built-in applications and the records of most third-party applications as well. This flag prohibits sensitive data from access by prying eyes. But beware: these records are not completely inaccessible to someone looking for this type of data, so do not keep any really sensitive information on your PalmPilot. Several secret-type applications are available that allow you to store such information in an encrypted format, for those concerned with keeping this type of information at hand.

Find

Although not an application, the Find feature deserves mention here. By tapping the **Find** button, you can search all of the records of all applications on the PalmPilot that support it. All of the built-in applications support this feature, as do many of the third-party applications that store data.

TIP

The built-in Find application will find only beginnings of a word; that is, if you are looking for "smoke" and type **oke** in the Find window, it will come up empty. Florent Pillet has written a HackMaster Hack called FindHack that addresses this deficiency. For more information about FindHack and HackMaster, see Chapter 6, PalmPilot Shareware.

PalmPilot Desktop

The PalmPilot Desktop is the PalmPilot Personal Information Manager, or PIM. Although not as powerful as other PIM products available, this Desktop software provides a seamless integration with the data on the PalmPilot. How? Most PIM applications have their own features and functions, and though similar from one to the next, each has its own way of doing things. In contrast, the PalmPilot Desktop was designed to mirror the data and structure of the applications on the PalmPilot.

Essential Features

The Desktop software, for the most part, duplicates the applications available on the PalmPilot. Each of the four icons on the left side of the window (see Figure 2.14) represents one of the four main applications found on the PalmPilot. Consequently, everything that can be done on the PalmPilot can be done with the Desktop software. In addition, the Desktop software includes some features and functionality not found on the PalmPilot, explored in the following subsections.

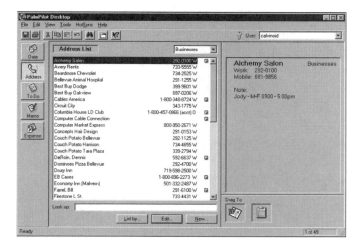

Figure 2.14 The AddressBook view of PalmPilot Desktop.

DateBook

The Desktop version DateBook application is perhaps the most enhanced of the standard applications. Like the application on the PalmPilot, it has three views, Day, Week, and Month. But the Daily view offers significantly more than just the current day's appointments. You can also see a monthly calendar and the current ToDo list (see Figure 2.15). And, in the Weekly view, you can drag appointments and drop them where you need them, as well as cut, copy, and paste them.

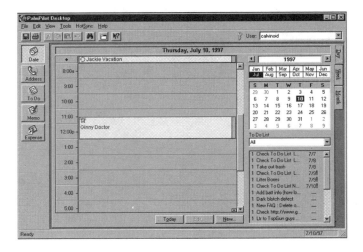

Figure 2.15 The Daily view of the DateBook screen.

Macintosh users out there should know that the Mac version of the PalmPilot Desktop program is almost identical to that of the PC version. To illustrate this, Figure 2.16 shows the Mac version of the Daily view of the DateBook screen.

NOTE

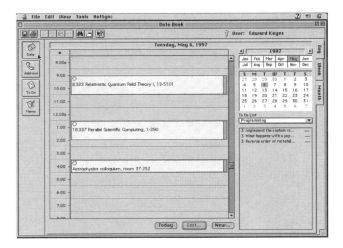

Figure 2.16 Macintosh version of the AddressBook Daily view.

The Monthly view offers a full view of the month, including the beginning text for all the appointments in that month, as well as appointments surrounding the current month. See Figure 2.17 for a screenshot of the Monthly view.

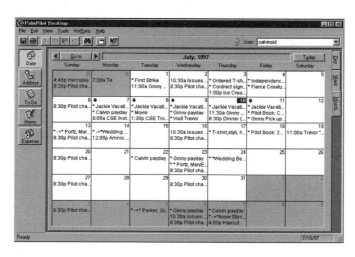

Figure 2.17 The Monthly view of the DateBook screen.

AddressBook

The AddressBook portion of the Desktop application may not appear functionally different from that on the PalmPilot, but there are a few hidden goodies there to be aware of. One of these is that you can drag and drop your AddressBook entries directly to the Clipboard and/or to Microsoft Word. To do this, simply drag the desired entry and drop it over the MS Word or the Clipboard icon at the bottom right of the window.

NOTE

To use the drag-and-drop feature with Word 97 (and the expense sync to Excel 97), you have to install the 2.1 update to the PalmPilot Desktop. It is available at 3Com's site at **http://www.usr.com/palm/custsupp/readme21.html.**

Another Desktop AddressBook feature lets you dial the phone number of any entry (Windows version only). To do this, highlight the entry to dial and select **Dial** from the Edit menu, press **Ctrl-I**, or click the right mouse button and select **Dial** from the pop-up menu.

NOTE For the dial feature to work, you must have the Microsoft Phone Dialer installed and working (which requires modem support). By default, this program is located in the Programs/Accessories Start menu. If it is not installed, you can do so by inserting your Windows 95 CD-ROM and going to the Add/Remove Programs portion of the Control Panel. From there, go to the Windows Setup tab, select **Communications**, and press the **Details** button. Check the Phone Dialer line, click **OK**, and follow the directions to install the application.

The AddressBook portion of the PalmPilot Desktop can also be used to import data from other AddressBook applications and/or personal information managers. This import function supports comma- (CSV) and tab-separated files, to which most of the other PIM and database applications can export. To import data into the AddressBook portion of the Desktop application, select **Import** from the File menu when you have the AddressBook button selected. After selecting the file from which you would like to import, you are presented with the Specify Import Fields window. In this window, you select the fields and order of those fields into which you'd like to import your data. To move fields to their corresponding input positions, simply drag the fields to the correct lines in the data display box. Figure 2.18 shows this window, with selected fields moved and marked for import.

Figure 2.18 The Specify Import Fields window.

NOTE

You can also import from archive files. These files are created either when you delete data in the PalmPilot, or when in the Desktop application, you are asked if you want to save your data in an archive file on the PC. Note that this file won't be created until the next time you perform a HotSync, regardless of whether the data is being deleted from the PalmPilot or the Desktop application. Archive files can also be created from the Desktop application by selecting **File/Export**.

ToDo List, MemoPad, and Expense

Aside from being able to drag items to the Word and Clipboard icons, the Desktop versions of the ToDo List and MemoPad are functionally identical to those on the PalmPilot itself.

There is, however, one more peculiarity to take note of: the Expense button doesn't actually bring up a window to allow you to edit the Expense data as in the other Desktop applications. Instead, pressing the **Expense** button results in your Expense data being brought into Excel.

NOTE

If you don't have Excel installed on your computer, pressing the **Expense** button results in a message stating that the information was saved as a text file; it also gives the location of this file. This file can then be imported into any other spreadsheet application, although doing so will require you to manually format the data in that application.

Changes to Desktop

This list reflects the changes from the 1.0 to the 2.0 version of the Desktop.

- You can now print Month/Week view.
- You can dial numbers from the AddressBook using a modem (which requires modem support).
- You can insert date/time with keystrokes.
- Using profiles you can load data into a PalmPilot without giving a user name for multiple PalmPilot scenarios.
- The ToDo List appears in DateBook view (see Figure 2.19).

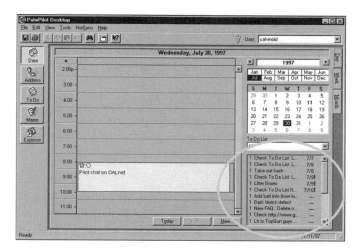

Figure 2.19 Desktop 2.0 now shows an abbreviated ToDo list in the DateBook Day view.

- You can now import a memo larger than 4K into MemoPad (by splitting the incoming text into 4K pieces/memos).

Graffiti

The method used most to input text into the PalmPilot is Graffiti, which is very easy to learn and use. Although most letters of the alphabet drawn in Graffiti are close to their actual shapes, some letters/characters are difficult to remember and others are difficult to recognize. Let's look at some tips to help in both of these instances.

Forgotten Letters

There are several good ways to remember those oft-forgotten letters, as well as some general tips for using Graffiti. These are:

- To help remember strokes, use the Graffiti Reference card, which comes in two flavors: a stick-on card to attach to the back of the PalmPilot and a foldover card to keep in the case or in your wallet/purse.

- The new PalmOS 2.0 includes an on-screen equivalent of the reference card. This screen is available from all the built-in applications, via the Edit menu. You can also define the Graffiti upstroke to display this, by going to the Buttons screen in Preferences and selecting the **Pen** button.

- The Graffiti Help application, written by Bill Kirby, does a good job of showing all the available Graffiti characters and the required strokes (see Figure 2.20).

Figure 2.20 The Extended shift page of Bill Kirby's Graffiti Help app.

- The section in the PalmPilot documentation on Graffiti has some good tips, as well as information on alternate strokes for certain letters.

- Use large strokes and try to write at a 90-degree angle.

- When in doubt, bring up the on-screen keyboard. Do this by pressing the stylus in the graffiti area and dragging the tip into the main screen area (this is the Graffiti upstroke defined in the Buttons screen of Prefs) or issuing the Command (the /) character and a **k**. New with Palm OS 2.0, you can also tap the lower-left or -right corners of the Graffiti input box to bring up the keyboard (left) or the numeric pad (right).

- Install the Grafaid program by Chris Crawford. This application allows you to see the actual Graffiti strokes after you've drawn them, as well as the text those strokes generate. You can also draw Graffiti strokes on the main screen area to help figure out what mistakes you might be making.

- Install the TealEcho Hack. This HackMaster application will echo to the screen any Graffiti characters you use, in any application. (See Chapter 6, PalmPilot Shareware, for more information on TealEcho and HackMaster.)

Troublesome Characters

Following are the letters and numbers that most people have difficulty with, along with tips for drawing their Graffiti equivalents.

D Make a loop, like a small cursive *L*, but backward (start at bottom right and end up at bottom left).

G Draw a *6*.

K Use the same stroke as the **D** just given, but rotate it 90 degrees counterclockwise.

L This is, for many, the most difficult letter to form. The secret to the perfect *L* is to start at the top-left corner of the Graffiti area and trace as closely as you can to the left and bottom sides of the "box." It also helps to make as close to a perfect 90-degree stroke as you can.

P Start at the bottom, and do not make too large an *O* shape at the top of the stroke.

Q This is the same as the **O** stroke, but overemphasize the tail of this letter.

R Follow the **P** instruction, but form a 45-degree tail. Here, too, a small *O* shape at the top of the stroke improves recognition.

V Make the stroke backward (starting at the top right instead of left).

Y Use the alternate stroke listed on page 25 of the documentation. This is basically an upside down **D** stroke, starting at the top left.

0 If you start at the top and make the downstroke on the left side, make sure the upstroke is at least as high as the starting point, otherwise you will end up with a *6*. It may help to write a *0* with an exaggerated upstroke, like the delta symbol used in calculus.

2 Write it as the letter *z*.

4 Write it as the letter *c* or *L*.

5 Write it as the letter *s*.

6 Make sure the loop is big enough, otherwise you end up with a *1*.

7 Write it as the reverse of *4*; that is, a reversed *c*.

8 Write it the same as the simplified version of the letter *y* (which looks like a lowercase Greek gamma).

9 Make the loop big and keep the downstroke vertical.

I credit Andrew Wong for the number hints. Another good source of help with Graffiti is Edgar's Graffiti Hints page, at **http://www.antioch.com.sg/edgar/ graffiti.html.**

Installing and Removing Applications

The PalmPilot documentation briefly covers the installation of applications, but be aware of the following options, especially if you're a Windows 95 user:

- You can use the INSTAPP program to install one application, then copy all the other .prc and .pdb files to the X:\PILOT-DIR\USER\INSTALL directory. A flag in the system registry of Windows 95 is "flipped" to indicate to the HotSync process that there are applications to be installed. If this flag is set, HotSync will install all applications it finds in this directory. You can facilitate this method by setting up the installation directory as a shortcut in the SendTo menu.

For more help on using the SendTo menu in Windows, click on the **Start** button, select **Help**, then search for **SendTo**.

- Use the PInstall program written by Mark Pierce to either double-click or (after installing in the SendTo Directory) right-click and SendTo one or multiple files for install at the next HotSync. PInstall sets the required flag in the Registry *and* copies the file(s) to the proper installation directory.
- Harry Ohlsen has written a shareware application that allows you to install all of your applications after a hard reset. Called Ripcord, this app also attempts to install applications to minimize memory fragmentation. For more information, go to: **http://wr.com.au/ harryo/ripcord/.**

- Eric Eilebrecht has written Silent App Installer so that you can set up .prc and .pdb files such that installing them requires only a double-click and a push of the **HotSync** button. For more information, go to: **http://ucsub.colorado.edu/~eilebrec/saip/saip.html**.

- Ain McKendrick has written Pilot Install Tool Pro 1.0, which enables you to schedule PalmPilot files (*.prc, *.pdb) for installation to your PalmPilot. The interface displays a list of all pending installs for a selected user, and provides Add/Remove buttons to update the list. This makes it easier to schedule repeated installs, as compared to the standard PalmPilot Install Tool.

3Com Service

3Com's service commitment ensures that PalmPilot owners can have their machines repaired quickly and back where they belong, in their hands. The PalmPilot has a standard warranty of one year on any defects (including the infamous stylus hole crack, and abnormal wear and tear of the Graffiti area, to name a couple of the more prevalent reasons for return). 3Com also charges a flat rate of $100 to repair a PalmPilot broken for reasons not covered under the warranty, or for those PalmPilots that break after the warranty has expired.

If you need to have your PalmPilot repaired, call 3Com at 1-847-676-1441, Monday through Friday, 8:00 A.M. to 6:00 P.M. central standard/daylight time. Whether the unit is going in for warranty repair or being fixed for the $100 flat fee, the service and turnaround times are the same.

Turnaround

The day (or two) after calling 3Com, you will receive a box from Airborne Express in which to put your broken PalmPilot. Send the box in, and, normally, within two or three business days, you will have it back.

Accessories

You can purchase various accessories to protect your PalmPilot, as well as enhance your use of it.

Cases

The case you choose is a very personal decision, and one person's perfect case could be the next person's hindrance. A few of the more popular ones are described in the following subsections.

Commercial

- *The Slim Leather from 3Com.* A small padded booklike case that folds over the left side of the PalmPilot, battery side, and screen area of the PalmPilot (the top, right, and bottom are exposed). It is closed by a small leather flap attached with a snap. This snap, because it is directly over the screen, causes concern that it could crack the screen, but this happens only in rare circumstances. A small pocket on the inside front cover can hold a few credit cards or notes.
- *The Leather Belt Clip case from 3Com.* A small, pouchlike case that includes padding and a protective barrier. Includes a Velcro closure top and a sturdy clip for attaching to your belt.

- *The Deluxe Leather from 3Com.* A large, trifold type case that is considerably taller than the PalmPilot (but once folded, only slightly wider). Made of the same leather as the slim case, it contains a notepad and several pockets on the inside front cover for carrying notes/credit cards.

- *Dooney & Bourke PalmPilot Cases.* Described by 3Com as an "elegant and luxurious" case made from all-weather leather, this is another pouch-type design, with a large flap that folds over the top, and a pocket for holding business cards or other small items. Includes extra protection for the screen area.

- *The Wrap/Wrap II/III/IV/etc. from the UK Connection.* A leather flipover case made of stiffer leather than the two 3Com ones, this case was designed with the intention of keeping it small and functional. It is attached to the PalmPilot in such a way that it doesn't have to be removed to use or HotSync the PalmPilot. More information on this case and ordering information is at **http://www.nwnet.co.uk/i2i/**.

- The E & B Company, **http://www2.ebcases.com/ebcases/html/ebhome.html**, makes a couple of cases for the PalmPilot. One, called Copilot, is similar to the 3Com Slim Leather, and the latest, the Pilot Glove II, has a flip-up cover that allows you to use the PalmPilot while it's in the case, and includes a pocket to allow storage of credit cards or other similar papers.

- The *PilotPouch from pilotWare* (**http://pilotware.marketmatrix.com**) is a canvas-style padded case. Other features include an outside pouch (for money, etc.) and a wraparound strap for support.

- *The FlipCase from Synergy Solutions, Inc.* (**http://www.synsolutions.com/ products/flipcase.html**) is a thin, flip-open leather case, similar in design to some of the wrap cases, in that it attaches with Velcro to the back of the PalmPilot, and you can HotSync the Pilot still in the case.

- *The Cockpit by Rhinoskin* (**http://www.rhinoskin.com**) is titanium, lined with neoprene. It hinges open to one side, allowing access to the PalmPilot's buttons while still in the case.

- The *Pi-Lid by Bzzt Company*'s (**http://www.artomatic.com/pi-lid/**) unique idea is actually more a screen protector than case. It attaches to the top of the PalmPilot, and the lid hinges down over the screen for protection. To use, just flip the screen up and write away!

Homemade and Other Off-the-Shelf Products

I've heard of cases made of everything from canvas to Zip-loc bags. Others use fly-fishing boxes, cases designed for the new slim Gameboy, and all shapes and sizes of premade cases that can be bought off the shelf. Again, the case you keep your PalmPilot in must meet your needs, so whether custom-made or handmade, the key is to find what works best for you.

Styli

To the best of my knowledge, there are two replacement styli for the PalmPilot; that is, one that fits in the same slot. Both are made by a company called PDA Panache, and they are a little heavier than the stock stylus. Some users claim they prefer the feel and heft of these more than the 3Com-supplied stick. Both styli are available in black chrome and gold, and include a plastic tip for writing on the screen. For more information, go to **http://www.pdapanache.com**.

If you just want to replace your stock stylus, a replacement three-pack can be ordered from most PDA accessory retailers and 3Com.

The alternative tools for writing on the screen that don't fit in the PalmPilot's slot are these:

- *Cross Pens (**http://www.crossusa.com**)* makes a "digital writer" refill for its line of pens ($5 each plus shipping. Call 1-800-ATCROSS to order; ask for the digital stylus refill).
- *PDA Panache* sells a line of styli designed for PDAs.
- *Pilot Pens* has a new Pentopia Line of styli (**http:www.pilotpen.com/ stylus/pentopia.htm**).
- *Kooky Grip* from .bak is a new ATC stylus that clips onto the side of the Pilot (**http:members.aol.com/dotbak/html/ kooky1.html**).

Screen Protection

Do you need a screen protector for your PalmPilot? Yes and no. A majority of PalmPilot owners use no screen protection and have no problems with scratches and or wear. On the other hand, scratches can and do occur, most often in the Graffiti input area. So, whether you use a screen protector for your PalmPilot is entirely up to you. Some people protect the entire screen, while others protect only the area that gets the most wear—the Graffiti input area.

If you decide you want to protect your screen, the options are as varied as the opinions on the value of screen protectors. Some of the more popular ones are listed next.

Commercial

- *WriteRight protectors from The Concept Kitchens.* These clear plastic film sheets come with a "low-tack" adhesive to keep them on the screen. They are very popular, but the main complaint is that they are somewhat difficult to install (for installation help, go to: **http://www.waysoft.com/pdainfo/pdapilot.html#right**).

WriteRight protectors come in full-sized sheets, so if you want to protect only the Graffiti area, you'll have to cut them yourself. A 12-pack costs $24.95, plus shipping. For more information, go to **http://www.conceptkitchen.com**.

- *DisplayGuard from PilotWare.* This is a clear piece of vinyl that you apply to your PalmPilot screen. Again, the main complaint seems to be the difficulty of application. Some report that smearing Windex or other cleaning solution on the plastic makes it easier to apply and work out the bubbles. One order of DisplayGuard includes one full-screen sheet and six sheets to cover the Graffiti area (three "paperlike" and three "glasslike"). Cost: $11.95. For more information, go to: **http://pilotware.marketmatrix.com/ Products/DisplayGuard/**.

- *Screen Protectors from Norman J. "Hunting Otter" Wilson.* Another vinyl sheet solution, these come in all sizes, from full-sheet to Graffiti area only. You can order these in any configuration you desire, with a minimum order of $5. Note that Norman Wilson is located in Canada, so shipping to U.S. locations requires going through customs and takes a while. For more information go to: **http://www.island.net/~hotter/ screenp1.html**.

- *PilotRite screen protectors, from PilotRite* (**http://members.aol. com/pilotrite/index.html**) have what the company calls "small, microscopic holes" that catch dirt and give a more "natural writing surface." Cost: $10, which includes a year's supply, money-back guarantee, and shipping/handling fees.

Miscellaneous

Here are some of the different variations and substances reportedly used as screen protection for a PalmPilot.

- *Scotch Tape.* Many people use Scotch Tape (make sure you get the #811, in the blue box) to cover just the Graffiti input area.

- *Post-it Tape Flags.* Another tapelike solution, again used to cover just the Graffiti input area. I recommend the large flags (2 x 1.7-inch, Style 682-1) and cut them to fit the entire Graffiti area. For an exact fit, measure the size of the Graffiti area, and use a word processor to measure and print exact templates on a clear laser transparency film. Stick the Post-it on the backside of the template and cut.

- *Post-it Notes.* Cut to cover just the Graffiti area. Tuck the portion not covered by adhesive under the case.

- *Transparency film.* A common full-screen solution. Install the film with the rough side up and cut it large enough to slide under the case so it doesn't slip. You can also take the case apart to install the film, but be careful not to damage any components in the process.

- *The vinyl solution* (used by a couple of the commercial companies listed) can be found at local crafts/hobby stores and cut to fit (for either full-screen or Graffiti input area).

Conclusion

In this chapter we've covered various aspects of the PalmPilot, ranging from the built-in applications to some of the available accessories. But, once you've mastered the basics, you'll probably want to extend the capabilties of your PalmPilot by using it for things like reading e-text and retrieving e-maill via a modem. We'll look at some connectivity and portability options for the PalmPilot in the next chapter.

CHAPTER 3

Portability and Connectivity

In This Chapter

- Data Portability
- HotSync
- Using the PalmPilot with third-party PIMs
- Electronic text
- E-mail
- Spreadsheets
- Databases and the PalmPilot
- Graphics
- Connectivity options
- Other modem/Internet applications
- Connecting devices to the PalmPilot

Data Portability

The PalmPilot's success is largely attributable to the ease with which users can synchronize data between their desktop and the PalmPilot. This chapter examines those applications that enable this *data portability.* As a preface to that, however, we'll briefly discuss how the PalmPilot achieves data synchronicity.

HotSync

HotSync is the main application used to transfer data to and from the PalmPilot. During a HotSync, a generic process takes place whereby the data for third-party applications is backed up. There are a few applications that supply their own desktop application and conduit, but most make the transfer of data possible by using the files that are automatically backed up to pull the data off the PalmPilot. These data files, created in the Backup directory where your PalmPilot software is located, are identified with the .pdb extension.

NOTE

The .pdb extension is used to identify those files that store an application's data. These files can be installed using the same method used to install files with the .prc extension, which is normally reserved for specifying applications.

NOTE

To meet the need for an easier method of transferring third-party application data, a shareware application called General Conduit Manager, or GCM, facilitates this process. See Chapter 6, PalmPilot Shareware, for more details on the GCM application.

There are two components to the HotSync application: The HotSync application that runs on the PalmPilot and the HotSync Manager program that runs on your desktop PC.

PalmPilot HotSync Application

The program that runs on the PalmPilot is the application that triggers the HotSync process. This application can be run in several ways, but the most common way is to place the PalmPilot in the cradle and press the **HotSync** button located near the cradle's base. Other alternatives are:

- Run the HotSync application on the PalmPilot, then select the **Local HotSync** icon.

- If you have the optional PalmPilot modem, press the button there to initiate a Modem HotSync

- Tap the **Modem HotSync** button in the HotSync application.

NOTE

If you are using a PalmPilot HotSync cable or a modem cable, they do not have the HotSync buttons on them, so you will have to start the HotSync process using the icons within the HotSync application.

The 2.0 version of HotSync allows you to specify which applications get synched when performing a Modem HotSync. This is done by bringing up the Conduit Setup screen, accessible from the Options menu. Use this method if you'd like to HotSync via the modem, but only to sync specific applications and their data.

Desktop HotSync Manager

The HotSync Manager program that runs on the desktop essentially just sits around, monitoring the serial port you specified to use with your PalmPilot. When it senses that the HotSync application on the PalmPilot is running, it launches, to supervise the transfer of data to and from the Desktop.

ROADMAP

For more information on the differences between the various versions of the HotSync Manager, see Chapter 4, Troubleshooting the PalmPilot: Common Q&A.

HotSync Manager is also where you specify the options you choose to use during the process, and in which direction, if any, to synchronize each of the built-in application's data. To configure this, select the **HotSync Manager's Custom** option. This window, shown in Figure 3.1, allows you to specify the synchronization for each of the displayed applications. The options for each are:

- Synchronize the files
- Desktop overwrites PalmPilot
- PalmPilot overwrites Desktop
- Do Nothing

While Synchronize is the default, any of these options can be set as the default for the applications.

NOTE

When the HotSync process "synchronizes" the files, changes made on the Desktop are reflected on the PalmPilot, and changes on the PalmPilot are reflected on the Desktop. The date and time of each change is noted, so that any alterations made to both will reflect the change made last after the files are synchronized.

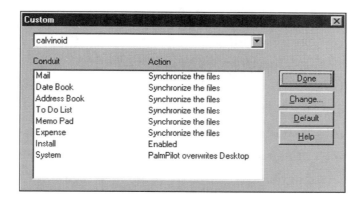

Figure 3.1 HotSync Manager's Custom window.

If you are wondering why you would want to use anything but the Synchronize the files command, suppose you install your PalmPilot Desktop on a second computer and want to start using it as the "main" synchronization machine. The first time, you would want to select **PalmPilot overwrites Desktop**, so that all of your information would be transferred to the new Desktop. And you'd select the same option if you decided to start synching with the first computer again, when you first performed a HotSync. Also, as you'll see in the next section, if you use a PIM other than the PalmPilot Desktop, you'd want these options disabled because the other PIM and its sync conduit would be performing the synchronization process for that data.

Other Personal Information Managers

You have the option to synchronize the PalmPilot with many of the more popular PIMs. If yours is not in the following list, contact the vendor to see if Pilot synchronization has been recently enabled.

- ACT! (**http://www.symantec.com**)
- Day-Timer Organizer 2.0 (**http://www.daytimer.com**)
- NetManage ECCO 3.03/4.0/Pro 4.0 for Win95/NT (**http://www.netmanage.com**)

- Goldmine (Elan Software) (**http://www.goldminesw.com**)
- Now Up-to-Date (**http://www.nowsoft.com**)
- Maximizer (**http://www.maximizer.com**)
- Microsoft Schedule+ for Win 95 (**http://www.microsoft.com**)
- Lotus Organizer 2.1 (**http://www.lotus.com**)
- Starfish Software's (Internet) Sidekick (1.0/2.0/95/97)
- Franklin Quest's Ascend 97 (**http://www.franklinquest.com**)
- Microsoft's Outlook (**http://www.microsoft.com/outlook/**)
- iSBiSTER's Time and Chaos32 (**http://www.isbister.com/ chaos32.html**)
- Okna Corporation's Desktop Set 6.0 (**http://www.okna.com**)

Most of these PIMs require a third-party program that performs the actual synchronization process. Contact your vendor for details.

Known synchronization products for these PIMs include:

- Tele-Sync from Tele-Support Software (**http://www.tssw.com**)
- Intellisync from IntelliLink Corp. (**http://www.ilink-corp.com/**)
- Now Syncronize from Now Software (**http://www.nowsoft.com/**)
- TrueSync from Starfish Software (**http://www.starfishsoftware.com**)
- Desktop to Go from Dataviz (**http://www.dataviz.com**)
- Pilot Mirror from Chapura, Inc (**http://www.chapura.com**)

A list of compatible programs is also available at the 3Com/PalmPilot Compatible page (**//www.usr.com/palm/pilosoft.html**).

How They Do It

Each of these synchronization applications has its own setup, layout, and data that it manages. Although each of these programs works with the PalmPilot differently, they all map their own data to data in the PalmPilot. That is, the PIM might use a field called Street to store the first line of an address, whereas the PalmPilot uses the field name Address to store the same data. By default, the sync program would automatically map the Street field in the PIM to the Address field in the PalmPilot, and give you the option to remap this to another field on your PalmPilot (application-dependent).

E-Text

The term *e-text,* short for *electronic text,* is used generically to refer to any text that has been converted to a digital format. Most PDAs include some capability to take any ASCII file and convert it to a form that can be loaded and read (anywhere you take your PDA) on that PDA. The PalmPilot is no exception.

On the PalmPilot, the conversion application is called Doc, written by Rick Bram (see Figure 3.2). Several conversion utilities enable you to convert any ASCII text file to Doc format, and this capability is supported on all major platforms, including Windows 95, UNIX, DOS, and Macintosh.

Figure 3.2 A screen from Rick Bram's Doc, the e-text reader for the PalmPilot.

57

For more information, including links to pages containing converters and e-texts, go to Rick's Doc page at **http://www.palmglyph.com**. Chapter 6, PalmPilot Shareware, also has more information on the various Doc conversion utilities, as well as the Doc application itself.

ROADMAP

In addition to Doc, the latest version of the Desktop software, 2.0, allows you to import text into the MemoPad application. Text larger than 4K is cut into 4K "chunks," each placed in a separate memo.

Importing text to MemoPad is possible only in the Windows version of the software.

NOTE

A few good Internet sites for accessing e-text files (including already converted files) are:

- MemoWare.com (**http://www.memoware.com**)
- Everything's Great (**http://www.teleport.com/~jleonard/**)
- Mike's Pilot Page (**http://www.geocities.com/SiliconValley/Lakes/7516/index.html**)
- The Lending Library (**http://www.mindspring.com/~duffmail/ lending.htm**)

E-Mail

Currently, there are several ways to compose, send, and receive e-mail using the PalmPilot:

- Using Palmeta Software Company's Palmeta Mail application you can route your mail from a supported mail program to and from the PalmPilot. Your e-mail program connects to your Internet Service Provider (ISP) and routes your e-mail to Palmeta Mail, which converts your messages to the PalmPilot MemoPad application format. Once your messages are HotSynced to the PalmPilot, you can read and respond to them using either the standard MemoPad application or Stingersoft's e-Mail app. Once your responses are ready to go, you can transfer them back to your ISP through Palmeta Mail and a supported mailer.

Version 1.7 of Palmeta Mail includes support for the following mail applications:

- Netscape Navigator v3.0/Gold v3.0 and Communicator v.4.x
- Microsoft Exchange, Windows Messaging, and Outlook 97
- Qualcomm Eudora Pro v3.x and Eudora Lite 3.0.1.

Palmeta Mail also works with many other e-mail systems, including: Microsoft Mail, Microsoft Fax, Microsoft Internet Mail, Lotus Notes v4.0/v4.51, and Novell GroupWise 5.x.

- The PalmPilot Professional comes with an e-mail application that is similar to Palmeta Mail in that both use the Desktop to receive and send mail via a supported e-mail interface. Note these differences:
  - Palmeta syncs to the MemoPad; USR e-mail syncs to a separate database and includes a conduit.
  - The e-mail app on the Professional is in ROM.
  - The e-mail app on the Professional is truncated to 8K (defaults to 4K, but can be changed in Preferences). Palmeta Mail chops long messages into parts.
  - As noted, the Professional app is in ROM, so only the Professional version of the PalmPilot has the e-mail application. Palmeta Mail works on all versions of the Pilot/PalmPilot.

- Smartcode Software, Inc.'s e-mail programs, HandStamp and HandStamp Pro, allow you to directly send and receive e-mail to and from a POP/SMTP server through the PalmPilot, without going through your desktop. In other words, HandStamp/HandStamp Pro directly dials your ISP and retrieves your mail. HandStamp Pro uses the built-in TCP/IP connection on the PalmPilot Professional, and includes a larger feature set than that of the base program; as such, it will run only on the Professional PalmPilot. For more information about HandStamp, go to **http://www.smartcodesoft.com**.

- Top Gun Postman is a freeware application that is similar to HandStamp Pro in that it uses the built-in TCP/IP application to connect to your ISP. TG Postman, however, also uses the built-in e-mail application to enable you to compose and read your mail. This application, too, runs only on the Professional PalmPilot.

- PilotMail is a service by which you send and receive e-mail via a Modem HotSync through the service. By setting up specially named MemoPad categories, or by using the built-in PalmPilot Pro (or the Pro upgrade board) e-mail application and calling the toll free number, your e-mail is synced directly to and from the PalmPilot (either MemoPad or the e-mail app). For more information, including access rates, go to **http://www. pilotmail.net**.

- You can also connect a modem to the serial port and directly dial your ISP using the application online. Once connected, you compose/send/read your mail online. This method requires that you have a shell account with your ISP, and that you be familiar with accessing your mail via this type of interface.

Spreadsheets

As of this writing, there are two spreadsheet applications for the PalmPilot, QuickSheet from Cutting Edge Software (**http://www.cesinc.com**) and Tinysheet from Starfort Software. QuickSheet is a limited-feature application that gives you the basic functionality necessary to perform basic spreadsheet functions on the PalmPilot. See Chapter 5, "Commercial Software," for more information on QuickSheet's capabilities and features.

Tinysheet is a shareware spreadsheet application that is even more limited than Quicksheet. However, it does hold a few advantages over Quicksheet, including price ($10), size, and speed. The limited nature of TinySheet, however, means that it will not suit the needs of those requiring a more robust application. TinySheet may be found at any online software site listed in Chapter 8, "Online Resources."

And don't forget, as mentioned in Chapter 2, using the PalmPilot's Expense application, you can export your expense data to an Excel spreadsheet, which includes several templates that format this data.

Databases

The PalmPilot you purchased does not include a native generic database application. However, several have been developed that you can install. Three are discussed here:

- PilotForms
- J-File
- MED

Forms for PalmPilot

Forms is a commercial database application designed for the PalmPilot by Pendragon Software Corporation ($49.95). Forms isn't marketed as a database program; instead it is described as a way to build "data collection applications" for the PalmPilot.

Here's the way Forms works: You build the form you want to use to input data into your PC, in an application called Forms Designer. You export that to the PalmPilot and use it to collect the data. Forms enables the use of several field types, including checkboxes, drop-down selection lists, and radio boxes. When you are ready to actually use that data, you perform a HotSync; then, via another application called the Forms Manager, you can view, manipulate, and export that data to an Access database, or to a format useable by Excel. For more information, go to the Pendragon Web page at **http://www.webfayre.com**.

J-File

J-File, a shareware application developed by Land-J Technologies ($15), is a simple generic database application for the PalmPilot. With J-File, you can define a database of up to 20 text fields (see Figure 3.3). Using J-File, you can sort on multiple fields, define record filters, jump forward or backward a specified number of records, jump to the bottom or top of the database, and conduct a flexible find. J-File also includes a utility for importing and exporting comma-delimited files to move data back and forth from your PC. Furthermore, a recent release of the General Conduit Manager includes a J-File database viewer/editor. Access the Land-J Technologies Web page for more details and the latest version (**http://www.shoppersmart.com/jlehett/pilprogs.html**).

Figure 3.3 J-File's New Database screen.

MED

MED, an abbreviation for Multiuser Editable Database, is a freeware application written by Rick Bram. MED closely resembles the AddressBook application that comes on your PalmPilot, except that MED allows you to change the name of any field. But the real strength of MED is that you can define a field as a pop-up, then assign the valid values for that field. Because it uses the same number of fields as the AddressBook, MED can import and export records to and from the AddressBook, allowing you, in effect, to use the AddressBook application to move your MED data to and from your desktop PC. For more information and the latest version, access Bram's MED page at **http://www.palmglyph.com**.

Graphics

Several applications are available for the PalmPilot that enable you to transfer graphic images, as well as draw them and store them on the PalmPilot. Unfortunately, because of the PalmPilot's memory limitations, these applications aren't as robust as the text-based applications just described. None allows you to bring your graphics with you, modify them, and then place them back on the Desktop to continue working later (unless you work only with two-color graphic images). Note that I only list the available applications here; I will describe them in the appropriate software chapters later in the book. To find any of these applications that aren't included on the CD-ROM, go to one of the software sites mentioned in Chapter 8, Online Resources. The available graphic applications include:

- *DinkyPad.* The largest and first of the lot, this application makes it possible to use virtual canvases and associate text with each drawing.

- *Doodle.* This app allows multiple pages and the use of varying pen widths.

- *ScratchPad.* This is just a simple program that allows multiple pages, no varying pen widths.

- *Scribble.* Another simple program, allowing for multiple pages. Available at PalmPilotGear HQ.

- *PalmDraw.* This drawing application allows you to move and resize pieces of your drawing, á la CAD-type applications.

- *HDSketch.* A drawing application with standard tools (line, square, etc.), but that also lets you move drawings to and from the PC.

- *TealPaint.* Another drawing program for the PalmPilot, this one also has the capability to move drawings to and from the PalmPilot. It includes a Fill feature (see Figure 3.4) and enables you to define drawings that are larger than one screen in height, á la DinkyPad.

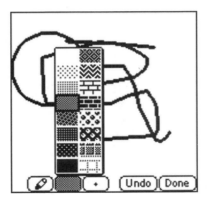

Figure 3.4 A screen from TealPaint, showing the pop-up fill pattern box.

- *SketchPad.* This very simple freeware app enables you to draw sketches and give them a title, displayable in a MemoPad-like listing.

Connectivity Options

Although designed to be used primarily with the HotSync cable to your computer, the PalmPilot now offers the option to connect to other devices. The most popular of these is a modem, whether the available clip-on modem for the PalmPilot, an external one connected to the PalmPilot using the PalmPilot modem cable, or the wireless Minstrel modem. Let's look at some of the available applications that use a modem, then briefly discuss the other connectivity options.

NOTE

The Minstrel modem from Novatel Wireless is a clip-on modem for the PalmPilot. Details concerning price and availability can be found at PalmPilotGear HQ (***http://www.pilotgear.com***).

Modem Applications

Without a doubt, the most frequently use of the modem is sending and receiving e-mail. But a modem can be used for much more, as this list attests:

- *Telnet.* Top Gun Telnet is a program with which you initiate a Telnet session with a remote computer, using the PalmPilot Pro's built-in TCP/IP stack.

- *Communications.* Online and AccessIt! are standard terminal programs. Online, which emulates a VT-100 interface, and AccessIt! can be used to dial any BBS or shell account.

- *Newsgroup readers.* NetNews uses the PalmPilot Pro's built-in TCP/IP stack to access your ISP so that you can read newsgroup articles selectively from your news server.

- *Web Browsing.* There are several Web browsers available for the PalmPilot. The upcoming HandWeb, which should be available by the time you read this, by Smartcode Software, Inc. (**http://www.smartcodesoft.com**) and PalmScape by Kazuho Oku are the two with the most features, while WorldFinder by Yamada Tatsushi is still in the early stages of development.

PalmScape is freeware, and is included on the companion CD-ROM.

**On the
CD-ROM**

- *IRC.* At the time of this writing, no applications are available that allow you to connect to an IRC session on your PalmPilot. Although the intensive text-input of IRC clashes with using a PalmPilot and its Graffiti input, it won't surprise me if an IRC client for the PalmPilot is available by the time you read this.

Other Devices

The PalmPilot can also be connected to various devices, including:

- GPS units
- Newton keyboard
- Twiddler keyboard

GPS Units

Flying Pilot is a flight plan application that, in addition to planning and displaying flight plan information, allows you to connect the PalmPilot to a Global Positioning System (GPS) unit and display information such as:

- GPS current magnetic course
- ground speed
- altitude

There is also an application called GPS tester, which allows you to display information from your GPS unit on your PalmPilot. GPS Tester displays things like:

- latitude/longitude
- altitude
- speed
- course

See Chapter 6, "PalmPilot Shareware," for more information on the Flying Pilot and GPS Tester applications.

Newton Keyboard

To connect and use a Newton keyboard with the PalmPilot, you must purchase the PiloKey package, which includes a software driver that accepts input from the keyboard, and a connector with which you link the keyboard to your PalmPilot via a standard cradle or Pilot serial cable. For more information about PiloKey, see PalmPilotGear HQ, **http://www. pilotgear.com**.

 For more information on where to find the FAQ pages on the CD-ROM, see the appendix, About the CD-ROM.

ROADMAP

The PiloKey application is available for purchase online at Landware (**http://www.landware.com**) and PilotGear HQ (**http://www.pilotgear. com**).

Twiddler Keyboard

Using the Twiddler keyboard, a one-handed, palm-sized chording keyboard (**http://www.handykey.com**), you can combine keys (or chords) to simulate the spectrum of a full-sized keyboard. The project to develop a software driver that supports this device is being spearheaded by Ed Keyes, at

Daggerware. For more information on the progress of this project, go to **http://www.daggerware.com/twiddle.htm**.

Conclusion

Now that we've covered PalmPilot basics, as well as the various connectivity options, let's look at some of the frequently asked questions (FAQs) that PalmPilot owners have.

CHAPTER 4

Troubleshooting the PalmPilot: Common Q&A

In This Chapter

- Common questions about the PalmPilot
- Usage tips

This is the most important chapter of this book, because it addresses the questions and difficulties many new PalmPilot users otherwise would struggle to solve on their own. The tips and troubleshooting recommendations given here are based largely on the Frequently Asked Questions portion of my Web site, although I also include new information. Note, however, that I don't cover application- or PIM-specific questions that are covered in other chapters.

 For more information about the contents of my online FAQ site, refer to Chapter 8, Online Resources.

ROADMAP

Common Questions About the PalmPilot

Q: *What is covered under the standard PalmPilot warranty? What isn't?*

A: The standard warranty for a PalmPilot is one year, which generally covers any problems caused by a defective unit. For warranty repair and related questions, call 3Com at 1-847-676-1441.

Common problems PalmPilot owners report that are covered under warranty include:

- Cracking in the case near the stylus hole (this problem is addressed specifically in a later question)
- Digitizer malfunctioning or needing recalibration (via Digitizer in Prefs) on a regular basis (see Figure 4.1)

Figure 4.1 The Digitizer screen. If you often have to recalibrate the Digitizer, your PalmPilot may need repair.

- Unusual wear of the Graffiti area
- Loss of data during a *quick* battery change (less than a minute)

The warranty does *not* cover any data lost due to the following:

- Any screen anomalies, such as unusual spots appearing under the surface of the glass
- Unit locking up or displaying erratic behavior

Problems *not* covered under warranty are:

- Screen scratches
- Damage due to user misuse or neglect
- Software-related problems such as fatal exception errors, screen lock-ups, and the like
- If your dog Spot uses the PalmPilot as a chew toy

NOTE

The list of problems now covered under warranty obviously is not meant to be comprehensive. If your PalmPilot is performing badly, call 3Com and ask to have the problem diagnosed.

Q: Is the 1 MB version faster than the 512 K version?

A: **Yes, the 1 MB boards do make the PalmPilot quicker (in all versions). The 1 MB board uses a 16-bit data bus as opposed to the 8-bit one found on the 128/512 K board.**

Q: Can the memory/ROM board be upgraded rather than replaced?

A: **Yes, but doing so requires modifications/additions to the memory board, and thus voids your warranty. Note that three options are available for upgrading PalmPilot boards:**

- *Pilot 1000/5000 boards (128K/512K RAM)*. These contain the 1.0 OS, and can be upgraded to 1 MB.

- *PalmPilot Personal boards (512K)*. These contain the 2.0 OS, and can be upgraded to 2 MB.

- *PalmPilot Professional boards (2MB RAM)*. These contain the 2.1 OS, and can be upgraded to 2 MB.

ROADMAP

For a more in-depth explanation of the differences among the OS versions, see Chapter 2, PalmPilot Basics.

The Technology Resource Group, Inc. (**http://www.trgnet.com/pilotweb/ pilot.html**) offers upgrade services, as well as an excellent upgrade FAQ, which goes into more detail about upgrade options. There you can access upgrades to 2 MB and 3 MB. And the more adventurous can perform these upgrades themselves, with the proper equipment. For more information, including a parts list and equipment recommendations, visit Steve Simmons Hardware Page at **http://web2.airmail.net/srsimmon/pilot**.

Q: *My Pilot has developed a crack at the top of the stylus holder. What are my options?*

A: **This crack appears in certain older PalmPilots probably because the memory door is not properly molded, and is pushing against that portion of the case. Eventually, this stress, coupled with the constant removal and insertion of the stylus, causes the case to crack at the stress point. Most Pilot owners never have this problem, but those who do are covered under 3Com's warranty and should contact the company for repair at 1-847-676-1441.**

Q: *My screen presses don't register. What should I do?*

A: The PalmPilot's touch-screen may need recalibrating. To do this, go to the Preferences application and select **Digitizer** from the pull-down menu. If this doesn't work, or you can't get to the Preferences (because the touch-screen is *way* off), try a reset. For more on this, refer to the tip on resetting the PalmPilot, later in this chapter.

Q: *The buttons on my PalmPilot tend to stick. How can I fix this?*

A: A number of owners of older PalmPilots report this problem. 3Com has recognized this as a manufacturing defect, and will repair/replace units under warranty. The problem is reportedly fixed on newer PalmPilot units.

Q: *Can the alarm be made to sound louder, or for longer? And is there a snooze feature?*

A: Yes and no. The alarm sound can be modified by installing an application called AlarmHack by Wes Cherry. AlarmHack allows you to change the type of the alarm sound (ranging from the standard noise to a chirping sound; see Figure 4.2) as well as its duration, but there is no way to make the alarm any louder, nor is there a way to give an alarm a snooze function. A "make-do" solution for a louder sound is to leave the PalmPilot on a hard, flat surface, which will make the alarm seem louder. AlarmHack also gives you the option to make the OK button the size of the entire screen, which is nice for turning off the alarm without having to look at the PalmPilot.

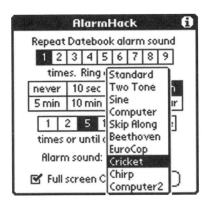

Figure 4.2 The AlarmHack application offers a variety of alarm sounds.

Volume Control App by Tan Kok Mun is another solution for altering the alarm volume. This application allows you to control various aspects of the PalmPilot's sounds. But note that there is some debate as to the effectiveness of this application, although most agree that it helps, if only slightly.

Finally, some "Piloteers" increase the volume of the alarm by drilling or melting holes in the back of the case, where the speaker is located. Beware: Doing this voids your warranty!

> *Q: I tried to install an app that wouldn't fit and now HotSync fails every time.*
>
> A: **When you use the INSTAPP (or a third-party program) to install an application, it is copied to the Install directory on your desktop (on a PC, this is the X:\pilot\username\install directory). If the application doesn't install properly because you don't have the available RAM, delete the application from the Install directory so that subsequent HotSyncs won't attempt to load it. Applications that install properly are deleted from this directory automatically by the HotSync process.**

ROADMAP

The directories located in the Pilot directory are explained later in this chapter.

Q: Can the PalmPilot be used to dial a phone number?

A: **No. This is one of the most requested features currently not supported by the Pilot. The hardware is incapable of creating the tones required to dial a phone. Actually, the processor can do it, but the low-pass filter and piezo speaker can't generate the required tone pair(s).**

Q: My PalmPilot is making noises! Is this normal?

A: **Yes, probably. There are reportedly four normal sounds made by the PalmPilot (three for all PalmPilots, one for the new PalmPilots). The first is a hiss or hum made by the voltage regulator; normally, this is loudest when the CPU is busy. You can hear this sound by holding the PalmPilot's back to your ear and turning it on.**

   The second sound, a tick, is made by the battery watchdog timer routine when it checks the sound circuit. This may occur every few minutes when you have System Sounds enabled.

   The third safe sound is a slight hum when the unit is off , this is caused by the PalmPilot keeping the clock and memory powered.

   And fourth, owners of the new PalmPilots may hear a slight whine when the backlight is enabled. This is caused by the hardware increasing the voltage enough to drive the backlighting feature.

Q: *I have to press buttons twice to turn on the PalmPilot. Can this be fixed?*

A: Usually, owners of early PalmPilot machines reported this problem. Installing the System Update 1.0.6 (which includes the 1.0.4 release) will fix this problem. Note that version 2.0 of the OS in the new PalmPilots includes all previous fixes, therefore owners of these should not have this problem.

   This problem may also occur on some PalmPilots when the batteries are running low. In particular, if the green button needs two presses, check the battery. See the Hints and Tips section later in this chapter for more information about when to change the batteries.

Q: *My PalmPilot won't turn on, or the screen is too dark/light.*

A: If you have recently installed the upgrade memory module or dropped the PalmPilot, the memory card may have become unseated as is causing screen display problems. For help with installing the memory card, refer to the Hints and Tips section later in this chapter.

   You can also try turning the contrast knob on the left side of the box, which may have spun off its setting when the PalmPilot was removed or put into the case.

   A third alternative is to do a reset. (Later in this chapter you'll learn how to reset the PalmPilot.) If this doesn't work, ask yourself whether you've taken your PalmPilot out in extreme cold or heat. There have been reports of errant screen behavior in inclement weather. Returning the PalmPilot to room temperature should quickly indicate if this is the case.

   If none of these fixes the problem, it's time to call 3Com to see if your unit might need to be fixed or replaced.

Q: I've just lost all the data on my computer/PalmPilot. Now what?

A: Before you initiate a HotSync to restore your data, make sure you start up the Desktop software, and under the HotSync menu, select Custom. Set the sync for either PalmPilot overwrites Desktop (lost data on the PC) or Desktop overwrites PalmPilot (lost data on the PalmPilot, normally due to a hard reset). Failure to do this will sometimes result in the appearance of duplicate records. The only way to eliminate duplicate records is to manually delete them.

ROADMAP

For more information on hard resets, including what they are and why you'd want to or have to do one, read Resetting the PalmPilot, later in this chapter. And, for help installing an application's data, read the answer to the question "Can I reinstall all applications (and their data) after a hard reset?" also later in this chapter.

Q: What are the differences among the HotSync versions?

A: HotSync 1.0 shipped (and still might be shipping on some really old units) with the original Pilot 1000 and 5000. It was followed by a prerelease version of HotSync 1.1, which fixed some of 1.0's problems (such as not backing up any application's data unless it was one of the first dozen or so apps installed). However, the prerelease also had a problem: Although it would back up all the applications installed on the PalmPilot, the data wouldn't be backed up on subsequent HotSyncs. The final version of 1.1 fixed all of these problems.

    The new HotSync 2.0 (which comes with the PalmPilots and Desktop 2.0) addresses all problems incurred with versions 1.0 and 1.1. (Most users have upgraded to at least version 1.1 HotSync by now, and they should access the 3Com HotSync 1.1 page at **http://www.usr.com/palm/custsupp/hs11rdme.html** for more information about specific issues with that version.) You can HotSync a 2.0 board with the older versions of HotSync, but you may encounter the problems that can accompany older versions of the HotSync program.

NOTE Anyone using both a new PalmPilot and an older PalmPilot with OS version 1.0 should be aware that HotSync/Desktop 2.0 works just fine with an OS 1.0 board, meaning you can install and use the new OS/desktop with both your old and new PalmPilots.

NOTE The new 2.1 upgrade to the PalmPilot Desktop comes with an updated HotSync Manager application, 2.0.1 (see Figure 4.3). This application automatically stores itself in the Windows 95 tray. This upgrade can be found at: **http://www.3Com.com/palm/custsupp/upgrade.html.**

Figure 4.3 The pop-up HotSync 2.0.1 menu.

The MacPac from 3Com now allows HotSyncing directly from the Macintosh. To date, however, only the four built-in PalmPilot applications are synced, along with third-party applications backed up to the Backup directory. MacPac was released without a conduit system because of design problems. Mac users who want to HotSync other conduits must either use SoftWindows (using the PC conduit system) or take (and port) the UNIX sync system.

A bug in the backup process on the Mac changes the modification and creation dates to invalid values. The fix for this, as well as a more in-depth explanation, is located at **http://www.geocities.com/Eureka/1943/fixpdbdate.html**.

NOTE

For performing a HotSync, UNIX users are actually in good shape, despite the lack of code from 3Com, which, is, however, being addressed by a substantial cooperative effort. The resulting code is located at **ftp://ftp.pfnet.com/pub/PalmOS/**.

Q: *HotSync was working but isn't now. What do I do?*

A: **Check the COM port. First make sure nothing else is connected. Then, in the HotSync Options menu, verify that you have selected the correct COM port.**

Some users have reported that if they use the COM port for anything else, they must close the HotSync Manager and restart it. This is normal.

A third cause of this problem may be if you use a laptop; your COM port may be going into a power-down state, and you may have to tweak the power-down options with the power management tools.

Q: *My MemoPad or ToDo applications won't sync, yet everything else does. What do I do?*

A: **To work with HotSync 1.0, a few third-party conduits "captured" either the MemoPad or the ToDo list. If these third-party apps were installed *and not uninstalled* they could have left behind the "traps," preventing normal HotSync transfers on these databases. To fix this, you can:**

- **Uninstall the application in question.**

For Palmeta Mail, deselect both the **Send outgoing mail** and **Receive incoming mail** options. If you've already uninstalled Palmeta Mail, reinstall it and do this, then uninstall the application again.

NOTE

- **Manually clean up the problem. In Windows 95:**

1. Click on **Start, Run**; type **REGEDIT**.
2. On the left-hand side, navigate until you find HKEY_CURRENT_USER/Software/Palm Computing/Pilot Desktop.
3. Under Pilot Desktop, check for any ApplicationX where X is 0, 1, 2, and so on. These are where the "traps" are placed.
4. Delete any ApplicationX entries to restore your desktop to its original state. (Note: You will also be disabling any of the third-party conduits you have installed.)

- **In Windows 3.1:**

1. Open File Manager.
2. Go to the Windows directory and double-click on **Pilot.ini**.
3. Look through the directory for a group called ApplicationX, where X is 0, 1, 2, and so on. These are where the "traps" are placed.
4. Delete any ApplicationX entries to restore your desktop to its original state. (Note: You will also be disabling any of the third-party conduits you have installed.)

Q: HotSync starts, but stops before any data is transferred.

A: This is a common complaint with HotSync 1.1. The solution is to reduce the baud rate. Most users report positive results at 19200 Kbps, but some have to go to 9600 Kbps.
The problem also occurs to users of certain laptops on which the PCMCIA modem and serial port both have to use the

same COM port due to limitations in the laptop system. In such systems, the serial port is recognized if it is enabled by the System Manager; but if the PCMCIA modem is still in the slot, no data can be transferred until the card is ejected. Then HotSync works fine.

Q: *Why does HotSync 1.1 back up third-party apps only once?*

A: **This is a problem with the prerelease version of HotSync 1.1. The fix is to download the final version of HotSync 1.1 for free from 3Com's HotSync 1.1 page at http://www.usr.com/palm/cust-supp/hs11rdme.html.**

An alternative fix is Pat Beirne's General Conduit Manager (discussed in Chapter 6), if you have it installed and are using it.

Q: *What are the "dot" shortcuts and what do they do?*

A: **There are several undocumented, built-in PalmPilot shortcuts that are accessed by issuing the shortcut command, which in Graffiti looks like a lowercase *l*, followed by a period (or "dot"), followed by a number.**

To issue these shortcuts, you must have an application running that allows text input, as if you were performing any other shortcut.

NOTE

This is perhaps one of the most asked questions, usually posed after users issue one of the more volatile shortcuts and subsequently have problems with their PalmPilot. The best advice is to read what these shortcuts do, and then use them with care. Known "dot" shortcuts are:

- .1: Launches some sort of "debug" mode, and opens the serial port, which can cause serious drain on the batteries if left open. Perform a soft reset to close.

- .2: Opens the serial port (another debug mode). Perform a soft reset to close.

- .3: Turns off auto-off.

- .4: Flashes user name and number. The purpose of this shortcut is unknown; what is known is that it will cause problems. **Do not try this one.**

- .5: Removes user configuration and HotSync log. Caution: If you resync after perfoming this shortcut, you will create duplicate entries! It is better to hard-reset, then PC-to-Pilot sync instead.

- .6: Displays the ROM date.

- .7: Toggles between NiCad/Alkaline. Meant for those using NiCad batteries, to show proper "fuel" gauge on the built-in applications' picker screen.

Q: Can I reinstall all applications (and their data) after a hard reset?

A: **There are several methods for installing more than one application at a time. Refer to the section on installing applications in Chapter 1 for more information. As to reinstalling an application's data, that depends on the application and whether it supports backing up data through the normal HotSync or its own conduit. If the application saves data to the standard Backup directory, simply initiating a HotSync after the reset will reinstall the data for that application (you'll need to install the application manually; see above). Mac users must run the FixPDB application mentioned in Chapter 6. And for applications that have their own conduits, follow the instructions that come with them.**

Q: What are .prc/.pdb files?

A: **The .prc files (short for program files or PalmPilot runnable code) contain programs intended to be sent/installed on the PalmPilot. A .prc file contains all the program's code, menus, strings, pictures, and so on that it requires to run. Usually,** a .prc file is self-contained, but on occasion you must also install an associated .pdb file.

The .pdb files (short for PalmPilot database files) contain data only that can be sent to the PalmPilot. You can send these files to the PalmPilot using the same techniques you would use for .prc files.

For those of you interested in more technical information:

- Pat Bierne's File Dumper utility can be used on PCs to view the contents of a .pdb file.
- Ron Nicholson's ypfile is a program that runs on the PalmPilot to display which .prc's and .pdb's you have installed.
- A program called Tides (by Ken Hancock) contains sample code that runs on the PC, and illustrates source code that produces a .pdb file.

Q: What is the purpose of the directories in x:\pilot (Windows)?

A: In the Install directory, you may find .prc and .pdb files ready to be sent to the PalmPilot. These files will stay here until they are installed onto the Pilot (at the next HotSync).

In the Update directory, you may find a .prc file that is the PalmOS update/patch that makes minor changes to the way the PalmPilot runs. (For those who have run both 1.0 and 2.0 of PalmOS, there will be two directories, one for each, that contain this .prc file.) For installation purposes, it's just another .prc and can be installed as such. For information about removing these system patches from your PalmPilot, see the related tip, later in this chapter.

In the Username/Backup directory you should find several .pdb files (see Figure 4.4). Certainly the Graffiti_Shortcuts.pdb will be there, but there may be others. It is in this directory that the HotSync process puts data it finds on the Pilot that it doesn't know how to back up (for applications that participate in the backup process). These files all share a similar format. As

.pdb files, they can be installed as any other application; but (of course) you must have installed the application that backed up the data to use the data contained in this file.

TIP

When you delete a third-party application on the PalmPilot, the backup on your PC isn't deleted. You can either leave these "orphan" backups there (then delete them from the PalmPilot if you ever do a hard reset) or delete them. I recommend that you periodically clean out this directory. (Set a repeating event in your PalmPilot to remind you!)

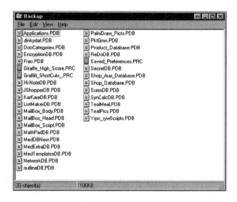

Figure 4.4 The Backup directory, showing a number of .pdb files (which I should have deleted by now).

In the Address, DateBook, MemoPad, and ToDo directories, you will find the data files used for the four main PalmPilot apps. These files are not in .pdb format; they are in .dat format, controlled by the Pilot.exe program (in cooperation with its conduits). Do not attempt to install these files as you would other .pdb files. (You can, however, copy them to another place on your hard drive for backup purposes.)

Q: When I tried to install an application, I got an out-of-memory error, but I know I have more than enough memory.

A: There are two reasons this might occur. First, if you are using 1.0 of the PalmOS and haven't installed the 1.0.6 PalmOS patch, you need to do so. Prior to the release of 1.0.6, the PalmPilot arranged data internally when it stored applications and data. As you installed applications and data into your PalmPilot, the information was scattered throughout available memory, often leading to fragmentation. Applications must be installed contiguously in memory. Thus, if you want to install a 24 K program and the largest segment of contiguous memory in your PalmPilot is 22 K, the installation will result in a "Not enough memory" error. In other words, although you may have 500-plus K of memory, enough of it may not be contiguous. PalmOS Update 1.0.6 alleviates this problem.

The new 2.0 OS version does not have this problem, but if you do get this error using PalmOS 2.0, it might be because you are running HackMaster and are trying to install a large application (or run an application that requires a large area of contiguous memory to run, such as HandFax). When a HackMaster hack is installed, it locks itself into a position in memory. Normally, this is not a problem, but if you install these hacks "here and there," you create, essentially, roadblocks that prevent memory from being aligned contiguously as it is freed. Fortunately, there is a solution (use only applicable items):

1. Disable all HackMaster hacks.

2. Deselect the **Always use Launchpad** option in Launchpad's Preferences.

3. Run the **Uninstall AlarmHack** menu item in AlarmHack.

4. Click on the **Uninstall** button in PowerFix.

5. Disable any other feature or program that may have set hooks into PalmOS.

6. Run HotSync again and your application should install, and it should be possible to re-enable everything you disabled in the preceding steps.

Ed Keyes, the developer of HackMaster, is aware of this problem, and is working on a solution.

Q: Why won't the built-in App selection screen scroll past the second page?

A: When you have more than two screens full of applications, pressing the screen up or down buttons on the built-in Application Selection screen will scroll only one screen. This is a known bug in early versions. To get past it, tap in the Graffiti area between each button press. This bug was fixed in PalmOS 1.0.6 and 2.0. You can avoid it entirely by using one of the third-party application launchers (Launchpad, PAL, etc.).

Q: What is the PalmPilot "tap" bug?

A: There are reports that tapping lightly on the screen of some PalmPilot 2.0 OS units produces random taps elsewhere on the screen. This bug can be verified using the TapTester application by Jeff Jetton. This problem is apparently the result of some internal changes made to 2.0 that were intended to change the screen sensitivity, making it easier to place the cursor on the left-hand side of the screen.

Since this problem was identified, 3Com/Palm has released a fix that is incorporated in OS Patch 2.0.1 (check the 3Com site or my main FAQ to find out the current OS patch version, which was 2.0.4 as of this writing). To determine which version of the OS (including patches) you have installed, look in the upper-right-hand corner of the Memory application.

Q: Why does my PalmPilot 512K/1024K show "Memory Used: xxx of 480/960 K?"

A: OS 2.0 doesn't include the system heap memory (a temporary work area used by PalmOS) when it lists free memory in the Memory application. Therefore, in the 2.0 OS, the Memory application will reveal "xxx of 480K/960K" instead of "xxx of 512K/1024K" (as displayed in the 1.0 OS). See Figure 4.5. The available memory is the same, however.

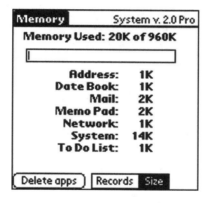

Figure 4.5 Memory application, showing only 960 K in a PalmPilot Pro.

Q: Why does a scheduled alarm cause a fatal exception error when the application that scheduled it is deleted?

A: If you delete (or reinstall) an application that has an alarm scheduled, when it is time for that alarm to go off, you'll get an error. The popular Digipet program is a prime example of an application that causes this. A couple of other examples are LookAtMe and BugMe.

Rick Huebner, the person who discovered this, is also the developer of ReDo. Here's his explanation of the problem:

When a program requests a wake-up alarm from the OS, it has to tell the OS who it is and what time to wake it up. Fair enough. However, the OS call for setting the alarm requires you to tell it who you are by giving it a database ID based on your current memory card address, rather than your application creator ID code, as it obviously should. When the alarm comes due, the OS tries to wake you up by using the specified database ID. But...if the app has since been deleted or reinstalled, that database ID may no longer be valid, causing an Invalid MemHandle error. Changing the time or doing a soft reset flushes all pending alarms out of the Pilot, and causes the Pilot to ask each app to re-establish any alarms it needs. Apparently, the OS designers weren't expecting any user-installed programs to use alarms for anything. Of course, it's no problem for DateBook, since it's in ROM and its address can't ever change.

Huebner's solution is to go to the Preferences application and bring up the Set Time dialog window.

Q: *Can I delete Giraffe, Expense, Mail, and other built-in apps?*

A: As explained in Chapter 1, the PalmPilot Personal comes with the Giraffe application in ROM; the Professional version and the Pro upgrade come with the Giraffe, Mail, and Expense applications also located in ROM. This means these applications are built-in, like the AddressBook, ToDo List, and so on. As such, they cannot be deleted (as a matter of fact, they don't even show up in the list of applications when you select the Delete apps button in the Memory application). However, because they are located in ROM, not RAM, they also do not take up any of your RAM, except for the data they store.

Hints and Tips

To complement the Q&A section, and to potentially forestall other questions, this section presents additional hints and tips that should prove of use to PalmPilot owners.

Batteries and the PalmPilot

The PalmPilot has very good power management routines built into the OS. Actually, the CPU is "sleeping" most of the time, even when you have the PalmPilot turned on. It wakes up just long enough to process screen presses, display the next screen full of information, and so on. Therefore, most applications simply do not use that much power. However, some do. Any application that experiences frequent updates to the screen (such as Klondike when playing in drag mode, DinkyPad, Reptoids, etc.) will cause the batteries to drain more quickly.

Figure 4.6 Launchpad can be set to show a graph, like the built-in application picker, or a voltage.

NOTE A problem with the newer PalmPilot OS 2.0 units causes batteries to be drained more quickly than necessary. To address this problem, Technology Resource Group, the same company that does the 2- and 3-megabyte upgrades, wrote the PowerFix application, which solved the problem but had to be run after every reset. Since then, 3Com has released System Patch 2.0.4, which addresses this and other known issues. For more information about this bug, go to TRG's page at **http://www.trgnet.com/pilotweb/Power.htm.**

That said, the average amount of time that batteries last is somewhere between four and six weeks. However, if you play any games, HotSync several times a day, or find yourself clicking/dragging a lot, your batteries might last only three weeks or less.

The PalmPilot's low-battery indicator will start to appear at around 2.00 or lower volts; the PalmPilot will stop operating at a little less than 1.00 volt (I've seen 0.79 mentioned). This means that on the standard application gauge, Full indicates 3.00 volts and Empty indicates 2.00 volts. If your PalmPilot begins to require two presses of the Power button to turn on, do not worry, it will still operate. Nevertheless, some recommend that at the first sign of erratic behavior you should put in a fresh set of batteries.

Other battery idiosyncrasies to be aware of include the following:

- The backlighting on the PalmPilot models reportedly doesn't cause a significant drain on the batteries during normal use.

- If you have upgraded your boards to 2 MB (or 3), your batteries will drain significantly faster than with the 1 MB/512 K/128 K boards. For example, if you were getting five weeks with your 1 MB board, you'll probably see about half that (two to three weeks) with the 2 MB board, assuming similar usage patterns.

- If your batteries are lasting only a couple of weeks, and you don't use your PalmPilot that much, something is wrong. Call 3Com about repair.

- If you have been playing around with the so-called dot shortcuts, you might have issued the one that keeps the serial port open all the time. The PiloKey application also locks open the serial port; this, too, drains batteries quickly. Do a soft reset to turn this off.

- If you are using Renewals (discussed in the next section), you should change your batteries somewhere around 50 percent on the meter. In line with standard alkalines, this usually is within two or so weeks, assuming normal use.

Rechargeable and/or Renewal Batteries

Rechargeable batteries can be used with the PalmPilot; however, exert some caution when using NiCad batteries, as they will work well, and then suddenly lose their voltage (possibly too quickly to back up your data). There is no backup battery inside the PalmPilot, so if you decide to use NiCad batteries, change them often and *always* carry a spare set. Also be aware that NiCads will discharge when they are not being used, so a pair that has been sitting around for a few days or weeks may not have any charge left in them.

Renewals, in contrast, work with few or no problems in the PalmPilot. Keep in mind, however, that renewals work best when they are recharged before being fully discharged. Most people who use renewals recommend that you put in a fresh pair when the voltage is somewhere between 2.3 and 2.5.

Installing the Memory/Upgrade Board

Before starting the installation, perform a HotSync!

1. To open the door, insert the blunt end of a paper clip into the small hole directly underneath the memory door.

2. Push in slightly, while gently sliding up on the memory door (use a fingernail to grip one of the little "feet"). Be careful not to push too hard with the clip; all you want to do is disengage the catch on the door, not pierce anything underneath.

3. Once the door has been removed, gently disengage the clips holding the old memory card in place, and lift it out. Insert the new memory card in its place, making sure that it's well seated (a chip that isn't seated properly is a common cause of many PalmPilot problems).

4. Gently push down until the clips engage.

5. Slide the memory door back on, making sure the catch at the bottom clicks.

General Tips

The following tips fall into no specific category, but deserve mention. (If you know of others that would be appreciated by the PalmPilot community, drop me a line at calvin@myself.com.)

- If you don't like seeing all of those blank appointment lines in the Daily Calendar view, you can configure the view to display only those that do. Or you can display only one blank line for days with no appointments. To make the change, go to the Options menu and select **Preferences**, then set your Start Time and End Time to the same time. Note: This is a Preferences option on the new PalmPilot 2.0 OS (see Figure 4.7).

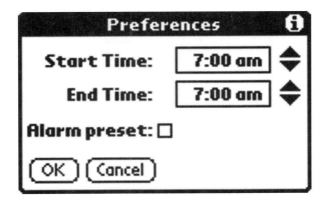

Figure 4.7 Setting the Start and End Time the same will eliminate the blank lines in the Daily view.

- If you know in which application the data you're looking for is stored, you can speed up a Find (using the silkscreen button) by launching Find from that application. It will be searched first.

- If you lose all power to your PalmPilot because of dead batteries, make sure to set the correct date before HotSyncing your data back in. If you don't, all the overdue alarms stored in your PalmPilot will go off at once. This also happens when you set the date of your PalmPilot to before these alarms, then change it back to the correct time.

- If you attach a note to a repeating appointment, you can choose whether the note applies to all occurrences of that appointment or to the current appointment only. A quick way to attach a note is to use the Attach Note command Graffiti stroke. Do a command stroke (lower left to upper right) and then make an A. This is used universally in all the built-in applications.

- If your better half has a PalmPilot, write him or her a little love note in DinkyPad, and make sure it's the first thing he or she sees when turning on the PalmPilot.

- If HotSync is timing out before it syncs your mail, try this before each HotSync: Hold both the down and up buttons, and tap in the upper-right corner of the screen. Tap **OK** on the dialog box that appears (see Figure 4.8). This turns off the time-out feature, and your Pilot will wait patiently while your mail syncs.

Figure 4.8 Dialog box shown after turning off the HotSync time-out feature.

- The AddressBook app provides four custom fields that you can rename to anything you want. If you choose to do this, be aware that renaming a custom field affects all Address List entries that use that field. To add custom information for a single entry without using a custom field, attach a note to the entry. Everything in the note will show up in the Address view, as if you had used a custom field.

- If you have repeating events and would like to modify the text of just one of them, try this: Go into Details for that record and change just one thing (mark it private, add a note, etc.). As you exit Details, you'll be asked if you want the change applied to all repeating events or just the current one. Select the **Current** button and the event will be separated from the other ones; then you can change the text without affecting them.

Another good source of general tips for the PalmPilot is the High Flyin' Pilot Page, at **http://www.novadesign.com/kermit/index.htm**.

Problems with IRQs and COM Ports in Windows

All Windows users have a mouse, normally on COM1; most users also have a modem, usually connected to COM2. If the modem is external, you need to add a new COM port; that is, buy a new serial board. If the modem is internal, you have a COM port you're not using. There are two ways you can use this port:

- Move the modem to another COM port.
- Move the unused COM port to another COM port.

COM1 and COM3 use IRQ 4; COM2 and COM4 use IRQ 3. The mouse cannot share an IRQ with anything; however, you can share an IRQ between your modem and the PalmPilot cradle. So, if your modem is in COM2, IRQ 3, configure your unused serial port to COM4, IRQ 3. Just be aware that you can't use the modem and the PalmPilot HotSync at the same time.

Of course the best solution, if it's available to you, is to install a bus or PS/2 style mouse. These mice do not use a COM port, per se, and are normally set up to use IRQ 12, allowing you to HotSync and use the mouse, and modem all at the same time.

PalmPilot Easter Eggs

Easter Eggs are little goodies that a programmer hides in an application. The PalmPilot has a few of these. One, the Taxi, isn't in PalmOS 2.0, so I've left the details about it off this list, but you can find this information in Question 36 of my FAQ. The other eggs are:

- *Development team credits.* Go to the Memory application, press the top of the screen and the **Page Down** button.
- *Error reading drive C.* Start the Giraffe application, press the top of the screen and the **Page Down** button.

- *Picture of two people.* Start the Giraffe application, press the lower-right corner and the **Page Up** button.

Figure 4.9 This picture is hidden in the Giraffe application. Did you find it?

- *Dancing palm tree.* Start the Giraffe application, press the **Help** button. Draw the pound character (#; dot, backward *N* stroke).

Resetting the PalmPilot

On occasion, your PalmPilot may lock up. Usually, this is because you loaded a third-party application that isn't performing properly. When this happens, you may see the infamous fatal exception error box, but pressing the button doesn't seem to do anything. There are three ways to reset the PalmPilot.

- *Soft Reset.* Press the **Reset** button (located in the small hole on the back of the PalmPilot (you'll need a paper clip or something similar). This will resolve most of the problems caused by errant applications. A soft reset is also supported by many third-party applications, including PAL, Agenda, PiloKey, HackMaster, and Launchpad.

- *Warm Reset.* Press the **Reset** button while holding the **Up** button. This will start the PalmPilot without any of the application "hooks" that normally start, such as OS patches, HackMaster hacks, Launchpad start code, and others. If a program is causing problems and a soft reset doesn't help, this may be the answer.

- *Hard Reset.* Press the **Reset** button while holding the green Power button. You will be prompted to confirm that this is what you want to do. Press the **Scroll Up** button to perform a hard reset. (Pressing any other button will perform a soft reset at this point.) Warning: Unless your PalmPilot is physically broken, a hard reset *will* work, but delete everything installed on your PalmPilot. Essentially, you're returning the PalmPilot to its out-of-the-box state. Therefore, use this as a last resort, and remember, as long as you regularly HotSync, you're okay. Before initiating a HotSync to restore your PalmPilot, be sure to fire up the Desktop application; under the HotSync menu, select **Custom** and set all the conduits to **Desktop overwrites PalmPilot**. This will restore all of your built-in applications' data; then you have to manually install all of your applications. If everything goes well on the next HotSync, those applications' data will also be restored (if that application performs a backup; some don't).

Deleting OS Patches

3Com/Palm does a pretty good job of testing system/OS patches before they are released; nevertheless, some users have problems with the patches and want to delete the new update to isolate which application caused them. One way to rid yourself of all OS patches is to do a hard reset, but that is not recommended. Here's the better way:

1. To disable system patches, perform a reset and hold the **Page Up** button (you have to hold it until you're out of the initial "Welcome to" screen). Now you can go to the Memory app and delete the patches as you would any other application. If you see System 2.0 (or System 1.0) instead of the normal System 2.0.x (or System 1.0.x), you did it right.

2. At this point, the patch isn't installed, so you can test whatever you want to uninstall. To make the patch active again, simply perform a soft reset.

3. To reinstall the update, simply install the update .prc file as you would any other. You will be prompted to reset your PalmPilot after the patch is installed.

Conclusion

Now that we've covered PalmPilot tips and troubleshooting, let's take a look at some commercially available applications for the PalmPilot.

CHAPTER 5

Commercial Software

In This Chapter

- Commercially available applications for the PalmPilot

In this and the next chapter, I introduce the third-party applications that are available for the PalmPilot. First are the applications that comprise what I consider "commercial" software. Chapter 6 covers everything else (shareware, freeware, etc.).

What is the difference between commercial software and shareware? That is a question to which one firm answer is hard to come by. However, for the purpose of this book, commercial software is defined as applications that:

- Are marketed by a commercial software company
- Include a manual and technical support
- Do not have a demo or "try-before-you-buy" version available

With those criteria in mind, be aware that there are deviations. For example, there are applications available for download on the Internet that do not come with a manual, yet they are definitely commercial. Likewise, there are shareware applications that appear to be marketed by commercial companies; and although these apps might have a demo version, you may not be able to fully evaluate the software before you buy it (one of the primary definitions of shareware). The point is, shareware and commercial boundaries are not always distinct.

Commercial Availability

All the applications described in this section are available for download and purchase from the Internet. Some are also available commercially, through mail order vendors and retail outlets. In the future, as the market for PalmPilot applications continues to grow, no doubt more of such applications will appear on retail shelves.

Software

The software application presented in this subsection are listed in this order: company name, company Internet address, version number available as of this writing, cost as of this writing, and a brief description.

Communications

HandFax

Company: SmartCode Software

http://www.smartcodesoft.com/

Version: 1.0

Cost: $49.95

HandFax allows you to send faxes directly from your PalmPilot. With HandFax, you can perform a phone number lookup, send MemoPad documents, store faxes and edit/send them later, design customizable cover pages (includes built-in bitmap editor), and log all faxes sent. HandFax can be used on any model of PalmPilot, and requires only the PalmPilot and a modem to operate (modem must be Class 2/2.0 fax-compatible).

HandStamp

Company: SmartCode Software

http://www.smartcodesoft.com

Version: 2.0

Cost: $49.95

Using a modem connected to your PalmPilot, HandStamp allows you to connect with your Internet service provider to send (with CCs) and receive e-mail. Because HandStamp includes its own TCP/IP stack, it can run on any model of PalmPilot. Addressees can be added from the built-in AddressBook application.

HandStamp is a solid program, and currently the only choice for older PalmPilot 1000/5000 and PalmPilot Personal owners who would like to directly connect to their ISP and send/receive e-mail.

Figure 5.1 Message composition screen of HandStamp.

HandStamp Pro

Company: SmartCode Software

http://www.smartcodesoft.com

Version: 1.0

Cost: $69.95

HandStamp Pro starts where HandStamp leaves off, by adding such features as message filtering, multiple mail folders, and full credit card number support. HandStamp Pro uses the built-in TCP/IP stack of the PalmPilot Professional, so only Pro owners (or those who have upgraded to the 1 MB Pro version) can use HandStamp Pro. Note that the HandStamp upgrade to HandStamp Pro (currently available only electronically) costs $19.95.

Palmeta Mail

Company: Palmeta

http://www.palmeta.com

Version: 1.7

Cost: $39.95

Palmeta Mail e-mail-enables the 3Com PalmPilot. With each HotSync, the software transfers incoming e-mail to your PalmPilot's MemoPad inbox, and outgoing e-mail (or faxes) composed on PalmPilot to your PC e-mail outbox. With Palmeta Mail, e-mail synchronizations place entire messages onto your PalmPilot (there are no arbitrary cut-offs in the middle of lengthier messages). Incoming mail is automatically segmented, based on the maximum size of a MemoPad item (4,000 characters). When you reach the end of a segment, just press the scroll-down button to continue to the next.

Palmeta Mail v1.7 supports syncing to and from the following applications: Netscape Navigator v3.0/Gold v3.0 and Communicator v.4.x; Microsoft Exchange, Windows Messaging, and Outlook 97; and Qualcomm Eudora Pro v3.x and Eudora Lite 3.0.1. Palmeta Mail also works with many other e-mail systems, including: Microsoft Mail, Microsoft Fax, Microsoft Internet Mail, Lotus Notes v4.0 to v4.51, and

Novell GroupWise 5.x. Palmeta Mail provides e-mail connectivity for all PalmPilot models and desktop platforms, including the original PalmPilot 1000/5000 models, the new PalmPilot Personal/Professional models, as well as the upgrades. Palmeta Mail automatically configures itself for correct operation with HotSync v1.0, v1.1, or v2.0. Now every PalmPilot user can have e-mail!

New features in Palmeta Mail v1.7 are streamlined install and automated creation of mailbox category names.

PilotMail Service

> Company: PilotMail
>
> http://www.pilotmail.net
>
> Version: n/a
>
> Cost: Varies with use

PilotMail isn't an application, but a mail and fax service for PalmPilot owners. With no special software, PilotMail allows you to send and receive mail using your PalmPilot and a modem. PilotMail assigns you an e-mail address, and since you dial directly, there is no need to go through an Internet service provider.

Because PilotMail uses the standard modem HotSync application to connect your PalmPilot to the service, the transfer of messages is much faster than going through a TCP/IP and mail server, such as the method used by HandStamp and TG Postman.

The PilotMail service costs $7 per month, in addition to a setup fee of $10 to start your account and an access fee of 5 cents per 30 seconds if you use the toll-free number (a typical call lasts 20 to 40 seconds). There is no charge if you dial the service directly or connect using the Network HotSync product.

Database

Forms for PalmPilot

Company: Pendragon Software

http://www.pendragon-software.com

Version: 1.1

Cost: $49.95

Forms allows you to create data-collection applications for your PalmPilot. It includes all the tools required to do the following: create custom data collection forms on the PC; install those forms on the PalmPilot, which will be used to collect and store data; transfer that data back to the PC into an Access database. You can then manipulate the data via Access or the Forms Manager. Forms is an excellent application for anyone who needs to collect and sync their data back to the PC. It also can double as a custom database application on the PalmPilot.

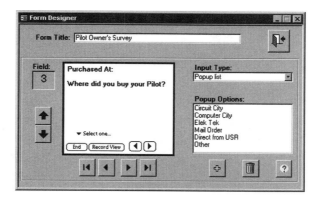

Figure 5.2 The Form Designer screen of Forms for PalmPilot.

Satellite Forms

>   Company: SoftMagic
>   http://www.softmagic.com
>   Version: 1.0
>   Cost: $495.00 (plus cost for RunTime Kit)

Satellite Forms is a custom forms development tool for the PalmPilot. You design custom forms on the desktop, which are ported to the PalmPilot, where data can be collected and transferred back to the desktop database. Satellite Forms consists of App Designer, PalmPilot Conduit, Satellite Forms HotSync Extension, Satellite Forms Engine, and manual. Pricing for the Software Development Kit (SDK) is $495. Call SoftMagic for pricing on the RunTime Kit, which is required to distribute or deploy applications.

Finance

ExpenseReporter

>   Company: Iambic
>   http://www.iambic.com
>   Version: 1.02
>   Cost: $49.95

ExpenseReporter is an expense tracking and reporting application for the PalmPilot. With it you can easily track your expenses by client, project, or type. ExpenseReporter includes a HotSync conduit through which you can transfer your expense data into your favorite spreadsheet or database application.

ExpenseRptr™	Wed 11/12/97	
Taxi Chase Visa		27.00
Show back to Hotel		
Meals Amex		138.00
Discuss bundle deal with Bob		
Supplies Amex		23.00
Photocopy datasheet		
Meals Advance Cash		12.00
Sandwich at show		
Dues & Su Direct Bill Compa		75.00
Exhibitor Badge		
Taxi Cash		27.00
From Hotel to Show		
(New) (Show...) ◆		**305.00**

Figure 5.3 The Expense Report screen of ExpenseReporter.

Financial Consultant

Company: Landware

http://www.landware.com

Version: 1.11

Cost: $39

Financial Consultant is a full-featured financial calculator application, whose capabilities include: time and money calculations, date functions, amortizations, and more. It also enables basic scientific functions and advanced operations such as mortgages and investment analysis. You could get a calculator that does all these things separately, but owning Financial Consultant means you don't have to carry an extra box, and you can keep that functionality on your PalmPilot.

SynCalc

Company: Synergy Solutions

http://www.synsolutions.com

Version: 1.0

Cost: $39.95 (part of the Hi-5 suite)

SynCalc is a fully algebraic calculator for the PalmPilot. Although it doesn't have a large number of functions (yet), it does have some features that make it unique. One of the most interesting of these is the capability to drag and drop numbers to and from the 12 memory locations (which double as the number keypad). Another nice feature is the expression entry window, which enables the entry of lengthy expressions. SynCalc also supports an unlimited number of parentheses and up to 30 user-defined constants. Syncalc is part of the Hi-5 suite, so the price listed above represents the cost of the suite.

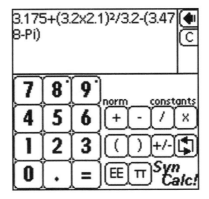

Figure 5.4 SynCalc screen. (Note the dots on 8 and 9; they signify that something is stored in those memory locations.)

Games

Reptoids

Company: Synergy Solutions

http://www.synsolutions.com

Version: 1.0

Cost: $39.95 (part of the Hi-5 suite)

Reptoids is a fairly accurate translation on the PalmPilot of Asteroids, an old arcade game where you navigate a spaceship around an asteroid field, shattering large rocks to make them small, or to make them disappear, if they are small already. Reptoids is available as freeware or as a part of the Hi-5 suite.

Graphics

QuickPad

Company: Landware

http://www.landware.com

Version: 1.0

Cost: $39.95 (part of the QuickPad suite)

QuickPad is a basic scratchpad drawing application bundled with the other applications in the QuickPac suite. It allows the creation of multiple pages, including captions for each page, which can be searched with the system Find routine.

Productivity

Athlete's Calculator

Company: Stevens Creek Software

http://www.stevenscreek.com/pilot

Version: 1.2.2

Cost: $14.95

The Athlete's Calculator is specialized for runners, cyclists, swimmers, and other athletes who need to track and calculate pace, distance, and other simple conversions. Allowing the input of data in a variety of units (miles, kilometers, yards, meters, etc.), the Athlete's Calculator is a must-have accessory for the PalmPilot athlete.

Figure 5.5 The Athlete's Calculator.

PilotClock

Company: Little Wing Software

http://www.lwsd.com

Version: 1.0

Cost: $19.95

This software comprises a full-featured clock, stopwatch, timer, and alarm application for the PalmPilot. With features including lap times, up to nine alarms, and easy-to-read large-digit numbers, there's no need to have another clock application on your PalmPilot!

My only complaint with PilotClock is that the Stopwatch and Timer applications "lock" the PalmPilot on, and aren't very useful if you have to time something for several hours. Fortunately, there are shareware applications that allow you to time events and that don't lock the PalmPilot on.

Figure 5.6 The PilotClock Stopwatch screen.

GolfTrac

Company: Fighter Pilot Software

http://www.fps.com/pilot/

Version: 1.5

Cost: $29.95

GolfTrac lets you track all aspects of your golf game on your PalmPilot: par for each hole, scores for up to four players, handicaps, and much more. Using GolfTrac, PalmPilot owners can track their running handicap, too. The software also features a course editor application where you can enter hole information for different golf courses. Finally, GolfTrac comes in a "lite" version in which you keep statistics on only one course at a time.

Figure 5.7 The Score Summary screen of GolfTrac.

Hi-5

Company: Synergy Solutions

http://www.synsolutions.com

Version: 1.0

Cost: $39.95

Hi-5 is a package of five handy PalmPilot applications: ListMaker, a generic checklist application; SynCalc, a fully algebraic calculator; Launch 'Em, a tabbed application launcher; Today, a tabbed interface agenda app; and Reptoids, an Asteroids-type arcade game. For more details, see the respective listings for each of these applications.

ListMaker

Company: Synergy Solutions

http://www.synsolutions.com

Version: 1.0

Cost: $39.95 (part of the Hi-5 suite)

ListMaker is a generic checklist application. On ListMaker's Common Items list you can define a list of common items for each task (each category, or list, has a separate list of common items). For example, you can set up a list of common grocery items for the Grocery checklist, a list of common household chores for the Home Maint checklist, and so on. Whereas the ToDo built-in list allows you to create only one-time usage checklists, ListMaker lets you use the same list of items repeatedly.

ListMaker is one of the five applications included in Synergy Solutions' Hi-5 suite. As of this writing, it is not available separately.

Figure 5.8 ListMaker's Common Items screen.

OnTap

Company: OnTap

http://www.ontaptech.com/

Version: 1.03

Cost: Varies

OnTap is a collection of software enabling you to build and distribute documents, via e-mail, to multiple users. It consists of an OnTap server that receives the documents, converts them to OnTap format, and disseminates them to a predefined list of users. The second element of OnTap is Reader, which allows you to read the documents on the PalmPilot. OnTap documents support the use of boldfacing, underlining, fonts, and hypertext links within a document, so that you can format your documents in an easy-to-read design.

OnTap delivers two product lines, Corporate and Personal. Corporate includes an OnTap Reader site license ($2,995/100 users), OnTap Server site license ($3,995), OnTap Support Agreement (not yet priced), and Custom Application consulting. The Personal product line includes the OnTap Introductory Bundle ($39.95), which contains one OnTap Reader, one Authoring Account for one year, the sample OnTap Demonstration Collection, and a discount on additional authoring subscriptions; OnTap Reader ($29.95), which is the simple reader application that includes the Demonstration Collection; OnTap Authoring Subscription ($19.95 per year introductory offer), which gives you e-mail access to the public OnTap server for one full year, allowing you to create and distribute documents readable with OnTap (note, you do not need this if you intend to read only OnTap documents).

QuickPac

Company: Landware
http://www.landware.com
Version: 1.0
Cost: $39.95

QuickPac from Landware is a suite of four applications: QuickLaunch, an applications launcher; QuickAgenda, a tabbed interface agenda display app; QuickText, an application that allows you to quickly add text to other applications; and QuickPad, a simple drawing application. For more information on these applications, see their respective entries in this chapter.

Quicksheet

Company: Cutting Edge Software

http://www.cesinc.com

Version: 2.0

Cost: $49.95

Quicksheet is the commercial spreadsheet program available for the PalmPilot. The initial 1.0 release was somewhat limited, but the latest release (2.0) adds several nice features and options, most markedly the desktop conduit and the slight upgrade to the user interface. Cell formatting and formulas are similar to what you'd expect in a spreadsheet application. My only complaint is that it doesn't take a very large sheet to slow Quicksheet down to a crawl. However, small, simple sheets are no problem, and quite speedy. If you need to be able to construct simple spreadsheets on your Pilot, this is a good option.

Figure 5.9 Expression pop-up list, showing available functions.

QuickText

Company: Landware

http://www.landware.com

Version: 1.0

Cost: $39.95 (part of the QuickPac suite)

QuickText is one of the four applications in the QuickPac suite from Landware. With it you can define sets of text to quickly insert in any application. To bring up the list of insertable text, simply double-tap on the screen, and a pop-up window with a list of text phrases will appear from which you select those to insert.

NOTE   QuickText and SelectHack shareware can coexist by setting SelectHack to its slowest double-tap setting.

Time Reporter

Company: Iambic

http://www.iambic.com

Version: 1.0

Cost: $99.95

Time Reporter is a time-tracking application for the PalmPilot, that lets you itemize time spent on a task, including details such as client, project, and task. You can set up Time Reporter to automatically keep track of time via a timer for each task, or you can manually enter the start and stop dates/times. The application also allows you to HotSync your data to the PC, and import it into a spreadsheet application of your choice.

Included in the price for Time Reporter is Iambic's ExpenseReporter application. See the entry in the Financial subsection for more details on that feature.

World Time

Company: Creative Digital

http://www.cdpubs.com

Version: 1.4

Cost: $25

World Time allows you to quickly display the time and dates in one of the 260-plus countries and locations around the world. A location can be found quickly using a Graffiti stroke of up to five characters. You can also define a set of special locations, which can be kept and viewed separately.

The World Time demo included on the CD with this book displays only the first 25 countries.

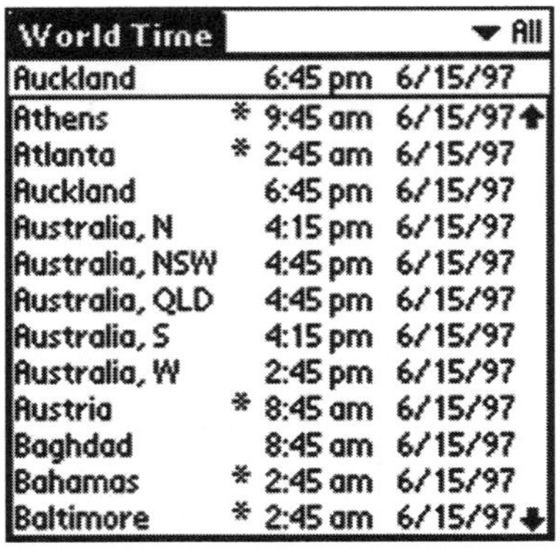

Figure 5.10 World Time.

Programming

CASL

Company: CASL Soft

http://www.caslsoft.com

Version: 1.0

Cost: $64.95

CASL, short for Compact Application Solution Language, is a full-featured programming environment for the PalmPilot. CASL has the capability to write the applications on the desktop and transfer them to the PalmPilot. In order to run CASL applications on the PalmPilot, you must install the CASL runtime file; this file is installed only once and is used by all CASL-written applications.

One of the more interesting capabilities of CASL is that it will compile your applications to run both on the desktop and the PalmPilot. This means you can update a database on the PalmPilot, then HotSync, and update that same database on the desktop with the same (compiled for Windows) application.

Chapter 8, "Online Resources", has more information on using CASL to write an application.

ROADMAP

CodeWarrior for PalmPilot

Company: Metrowerks
http://www.metrowerks.com
Version: DR3
Cost: $369

Metrowerks' CodeWarrior for PalmPilot is the commercial C programming environment for the PalmPilot. Available for both Macintosh and Windows 95/NT platforms, this package consists of an integrated development environment (IDE), including an editor, a 68 K plug-in compiler and linker, a source-level debugger, the new direct-to-device debugger, and the new visual interface design editor (Constructor for PalmPilot). Metrowerks also offers CodeWarrior for PalmPilot software with a PalmPilot (either Personal or Professional model) for a special bundled price. Go to the Metrowerks Web page for more details on current bundles and pricing.

Utilities

Launch 'Em

Company: Synergy Solutions
http://www.synsolutions.com
Version: 1.0
Cost: $39.95 (part of the Hi-5 suite)

This is Eric Kenslow's LaunchPad application, renamed to be included with the Hi-5 suite from Synergy Solutions. Refer to the LaunchPad entry in the shareware chapter for a description of Launch 'Em.

Figure 5.11 Launch 'Em gives you a tabbed interface from which to select applications.

PiloKey

Company: Landware

http://www.landware.com

Version: 1.0

Cost: $39.95

With PiloKey you use a Newton keyboard to type text on your PalmPilot. Although this isn't something you'd use to scribble a quick ToDo or AddressBook entry, it comes in handy if and when you use the PalmPilot for composing notes and e-mail messages. The new PiloKey package, which is also available from PilotGear HQ, includes the software and the connector that allows you to attach the Newton keyboard to either the HotSync cradle or a HotSync cable.

When the PiloKey application is running, it takes over the serial port (and affects battery life), so you must turn it off in order to perform a

HotSync or use your modem. Two complaints about PiloKey are, first, that it requires you to do a soft-reset in order to disable the program, and, second, the price. With a keyboard costing around $80 to start with, and this package costing just under $40, using a Newton keyboard with the PalmPilot is not a cheap input alternative.

QuickAgenda

Company: Landware
http://www.landware.com
Version: 1.0
Cost: $39.95

QuickAgenda is virtually the same as the shareware application Agenda, renamed and packaged with a few other apps into the QuickPac suite. QuickAgenda adds no functionality to the Agenda program, save the pop-up menu for switching to other QuickPac applications. Read the description of Agenda in the next chapter for more details.

QuickLaunch

Company: Landware
http://www.landware.com
Version: 1.0
Cost: $39.95 (part of the QuickPac suite)

QuickLaunch is essentially the same as the shareware application PAL, renamed and packaged with a few other apps into the QuickPac suite.

QuickLaunch adds no functionality to the PAL program, save the pop-up menu for switching to other QuickPac applications. Read the description of PAL in the next chapter for more details.

Today

Company: Synergy Solutions

http://www.synsolutions.com

Version: 1.0

Cost: $39.95 (part of the QuickPac suite)

Today is a tabbed interface agenda application, with three tabs that allow you to view upcoming appointments and ToDo items for today, tomorrow, and the upcoming week. Tapping on an entry in any of the screens will take you directly to that item in the corresponding application.

Figure 5.12 Today's Week tab screen.

Conclusion

You'll discover that the number of commercial applications for the PalmPilot pales in comparison to the available shareware and freeware applications, but as more commercial companies realize the market potential of the PalmPilot, this will change. With reportedly 1 million (or more) PalmPilot users, there is a growing market yet to be tapped by the commercial software industry.

And, though most applications currently available tend to fall under the productivity category, we may begin to see more diversity in the types of applications that become available as well. The two recent PalmPilot "suites," which give users a broad base of productivity, utility, and game applications, are perhaps the first indicators of this trend.

CHAPTER 6

PalmPilot Shareware and Freeware

In This Chapter

- Shareware and freeware applications available for the PalmPilot

This chapter complements the previous, "Commercial Software", by describing a cross-section of shareware and freeware applications available for the PalmPilot, highlighted by those I consider essential for all PalmPilot owners. This list necessarily comprises only the best of the breed, for shareware and freeware applications for the PalmPilot are being released at a breakneck pace, a trend that shows no signs of abating.

Specifically, this chapter describes the 140-plus applications, which also appear on the book's companion CD-ROM. In addition, I've included descriptions for several other applications that I feel deserve mention. Those not included were left out for reasons of space restrictions, unavailability at time of this writing, or simply because of an oversight on my part. To locate other applications not featured in this book, go to the PalmPilotGear HQ, Ray's Pilot Archive, or Stingersoft Web sites. The URLs for these sites are listed in the Online Resources chapter.

Shareware and Freeware Categories

Applications listed in this chapter have been divided into the following categories:

- *Calculator.* Calculator or calculator-like applications.
- *cbasPad.* Applications written in cbasPad.
- *Communications.* Applications that use or require a modem.
- *Database.* Apps that store your data on the Pilot.
- *Demos.* Neat applications that deserve a look-see.
- *Desktop.* Applications that run on the desktop.
- *Finance.* Applications that deal with financial or business data.
- *Games.* Need I say more?
- *Graphics.* Drawing and CAD-like apps.
- *HackMaster Hacks.* HackMaster extensions.
- *Miscellaneous.* A conglomeration of apps without a home.
- *Productivity.* Applications that improve your work habits and help you save time.
- *Programming.* Programming tools and applications.
- *Utilities.* Add-ons, extensions, and other helpful applications.

NOTE

Although every effort was made to place applications in their proper category, some proved to be cross-over apps, so you may not agree with their placement. Fortunately, this won't affect their value.

Calculator

Abacus

**On the
CD-ROM**

Author: Matt Peterson

URL: http://www.dovcom.com

Version: 0.85b

Type: Shareware

Cost: $12.00

Abacus is a financial calculator based on the HP-12C model. As such, it is RPN-based, so if you like this type of calculator, and specifically, are used to the HP-12C, take a look at Abacus.

Figure 6.1 Abacus from Dovcom.

AlCalc

**On the
CD-ROM**

Author: Alan Weiner

URL: http://www.ajw.com

Version: 0.0.116a

Type: Shareware

Cost: $15.00

AlCalc is a fairly flexible calculator that features 38 decimal digits of precision, scrolling display, multiple number bases, and many more. Alan Weiner is a fan of calculators and so decided to use his programming skills to write a calculator app that did everything he wanted in a calculator. As such, AlCalc is very programmer-oriented. Its flexibility is demonstrated by the keypad's capability to change based on the mode you are in (Octal shows only 1-8, Binary has 1 and 0, etc.). Of course, it has standard conversion from one base to the next, and operations like AND, OR, XOR, and NOT. AlCalc is a great calculator, especially if you are a programmer.

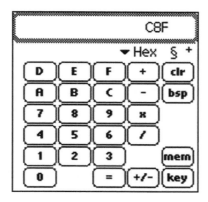

Figure 6.2 The keys change according to the mode in AlCalc.

BinCalc

**On the
CD-ROM**

Author: John Muth

URL: http://www.pilotsoft.com

Version: 1.01

Type: Shareware

Cost: $17.00

BinCalc is another RPN-style calculator written with the programmer in mind. It has the standard programmer functions, such as base conversion and logical operations, and features selectable word size, signed and unsigned operation, and a 10-element memory. BinCalc deserves a good look.

CurrCalc

**On the
CD-ROM**

Author: Bozidar Benc

URL: http://www.flash.net/home/k/e/kenw/bbenc/

Version: 1.04b

Type: Shareware

Cost: $10.00

CurrCalc is both a standard calculator and a currency-conversion calculator. Its standard features include most operations you'd expect: square root, square, and 1/x. But CurrCalc shines in its capability to do conversions. The application makes it possible to convert to and from any standard unit of measure (gallons, kilograms, pounds, etc.), including currency; you can also set your own units and conversion rates. CurrCalc also has a local/home time clock, and can be registered at PalmPilotGear HQ.

Figure 6.3 CurrCalc's conversion selection list.

Kalk

On the
CD-ROM

Author: Holger Klawitter

URL: http://www.math.uni-muenster.de/math/inst/ info/u/holger/ pilot.html

Version: 1.0.0

Type: Freeware

Cost: N/A

Kalk is a simple, RPN-like calculator for the PalmPilot with a full complement of mathematical and statistical functions. Though not as configurable as RPN, Kalk is a fine calculator for someone that is willing (or who likes/prefers) to use its RPN interface.

MathPad

On the
CD-ROM

Author: Rick Huebner

URL: http://www.probe.net/~rhuebner/mathpad.html

Version: 1.01

Type: Shareware

Cost: Varies

Although I categorized MathPad as a calculator, it is more a cross between a calculator and the MemoPad application. MathPad allows you to place mathematic formulas and expressions in a memo format and evaluate them, supply values for known variables, and solve for the unknowns, without having to rearrange the equation. Each memo stores its own variables and formulas, so you can easily maintain separate memos to calculate a wide variety of useful expressions.

MathPad can be registered for as little as $10.00 by mail or First Virtual (a registration service that you use a credit card to purchase items on the internet). Registrations handled by Kagi and PalmPilotGear HQ cost $11.50 and $11.95, respectively. See the Web page for more details on how to register online.

MetriCalc

Author: Jeremy Laurenson
URL: http://pilot.cc-inc.com/stinger/stingersoft.cfm
Version: 0.2b
Type: Freeware
Cost: N/A

MetriCalc is a calculator application that enables the standard operations, but is geared more toward unit conversions. Users can easily convert from one unit to another, simply by entering a number and pressing a couple of buttons. For instance, to determine how many ounces are in 2.13 gallons, you would enter **2.13**, press the **Gallons** button, then press the **Ounces** button (answer: 272.59391). Other applications provide this same functionality, but none in a format this easy. This is a highly recommended application.

RPN

Author: Russell Y. Webb

URL: http://kale.ee.cornell.edu/pilot/rpnMain.html

Version: 2.32

Type: Shareware

Cost: $15.00

RPN is the extremely popular and powerful Reverse Polish Notation calculator by Russell Webb. RPN is highly programmable, and includes its own set of programming byte codes. Several useful functions written for RPN include trig functions, logs and powers, conversion scripts, base functions, time calculations, checkbook, clock, and others. RPN is so popular that several shareware and freeware add-ons have been written for it, including AIR, FinFunctions, and NPV/IRR functions. If you don't mind (or prefer) using an RPN calculator, then RPN is for you!

Sums

Author: Andreas Linke

URL: http://www.tphys.uni-heidelberg.de/~linke/pilot/sums.html

Version: 1.4

Type: Freeware

Cost: N/A

Originally, Sums was written to provide a generic scorepad application for games and other activities that require a list of names and number to total. Subsequently, support was added for floating point numbers, almost making Sums a simple spreadsheet application (well, at least for adding and subtracting). Any need to keep a running total of numbers or scores can be satisfied using Sums.

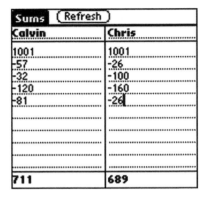

Figure 6.4 Sums is a good generic scorepad application.

cbasPad

AaGradient

Author: Jim Thompson

URL: http://www.telusplanet.net/public/jthompso/pilot.htm

Version: 1.0

Type: Freeware

Cost: N/A

This application for medical professionals calculates the P(A-a) difference from arterial blood gas results. You must change the barometric pressure to your altitude in line 80, and should verify results before using this program for patient care. AGB comes in source format only (text), so you'll have to convert it to a .pdb file using one of the utilities written by Tan Kok Mun, or cut/paste it from the MemoPad. Instructions on how to install basic programs are listed at Tan Kok Mun's page at **http://home1.pacific.net.sg/ ~kokmun/basic.htm**.

Arterial Blood Gasses (ABG)

On the CD-ROM

Author: Matt DeCaro

URL: http://home.pacific.net.sg/~kokmun/basic.htm

Version: 1.0

Type: Freeware

Cost: N/A

This BASIC program is used to analyze arterial blood gasses. It is small enough so that you should be able to easily cut/paste the program from MemoPad into a cbasPad window.

Basic Game Pack

On the CD-ROM

Author: Tan Kok Mun

URL: http://home.pacific.net.sg/~kokmun/basic.htm

Version: 21may

Type: Freeware

Cost: N/A

The Basic Game Pack consists of four simple games written using cbasPad: Ace2Hearts, DigitGuess, Flip, and Hangman. While limited by the cbasPad interface, and therefore not as fancy as some other games available for the PalmPilot, these are entertaining nonetheless. As with any cbasPad application, these programs provide sample code for anyone who wants to learn to write simple programs on the Pilot using cbasPad. This app has complete installation instructions, along with the required mbaspdb application, a utility used to append one cbasPad .pdb data file to another.

Figure 6.5 Games available in the Basic Game Pack.

Boxes

**On the
CD-ROM**

Author: Neil Fred Picciotto

URL: http://home.pacific.net.sg/~kokmun/basic.htm

Version: 1.1

Type: Freeware

Cost: N/A

Boxes is a nifty little cbasPad game that pits two players against one another in a game of strategy. Each player draws a line connecting two dots, and for every line that completes a square, the player scores his or her initial in that box. The person with the most boxes at the end of the game wins.

cbasPad PDB Utility Collection

**On the
CD-ROM**

Author: Tan Kok Mun

URL: http://home.pacific.net.sg/~kokmun/basic.htm

Version: 1.2

Type: Freeware

Cost: N/A

Figure 6.5 shows the utility programs, written in BASIC, that are included in the collection. There are conversion applications for length, temp, weight, and volume, as well as a wind chill calculator and credit card validator. As with other cbasPad applications, these give anyone interested in programming with cbasPad a good base of examples to work from; and the credit card application provides an interesting algorithm used to validate credit card numbers.

Figure 6.6 Programs available in the cbasPad Utility Collection.

Dots

On the CD-ROM

Author: Neil Fred Picciotto

URL: http://home.pacific.net.sg/~kokmun/basic.htm

Version: 1.2

Type: Freeware

Cost: N/A

In this unique cbasPad game, one player attempts to draw a line, one position at a time, from one side of the screen to the other while another player tries to prevent him or her from doing so. An interesting and fun game written in BASIC.

Drug Dosage

**On the
CD-ROM**

Author: Jim Thompson

URL: http://www.telusplanet.net/public/jthompso/pilot.htm

Version: 1.0

Type: Freeware

Cost: N/A

A cbasPad application used to calculate drug dosages for Erythromycin, Amoxicillin, and Septra. Each dosage calculator is a separate program, and all three are small enough to easily cut and paste from your MemoPad application (after pasting them there on the Desktop).

FeNACalc

**On the
CD-ROM**

Author: Jeff Schussler, MD

URL: http://home.pacific.net.sg/~kokmun/basic.htm

Version: 1.0

Type: Freeware

Cost: N/A

This cbasPad application calculates the fractional excretion of sodium.

Money Calculator Collection

**On the
CD-ROM**

Author: Tan Kok Mun

URL: http://home1.pacific.net.sg/~kokmun/basic.htm

Version: 2.01

Type: Freeware

Cost: N/A

The Money Calculator Collection features common financial applications, packaged in a .pdb file for easy loading. The archive includes the mbaspdb application that enables you to merge .pdb files if you have other cbasPad applications.

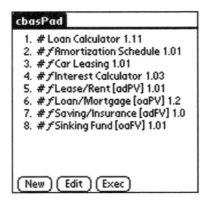

Figure 6.7 The various applications in the Money Calculator Collection for cbasPad.

MusicBox

On the CD-ROM

Author: Tan Kok Mun

URL: http://home1.pacific.net.sg/~kokmun/basic.htm

Version: 2.01

Type: Freeware

Cost: N/A

MusicBox plays prewritten tunes. Following the directions in the documentation, you can construct a song in the MemoPad application, specify that song when you run MusicBox, which will then load and play it. Certainly not a fancy application, MusicBox makes creating music fairly simple, and provides some good programming examples for those interested in writing cbasPad applications.

Pharmacy Calculations

On the CD-ROM

Author: David Watson

URL: http://home.pacific.net.sg/~kokmun/basic.htm

Version: 1.1

Type: Freeware

Cost: N/A

These cbasPad programs will calculate Creatinine clearance, ideal body weight, and body surface area when given the patient's weight, height, age, serum Creatinine, and sex. The file RxCalc1 (in the archive) uses pounds and inches; the newer file, RxCalc1m, uses kilograms and centimeters.

Communications

DBFax

> Author: David Bertrand
>
> URL: http://www.cybermail.net/~dbertran/faxpage.htm
>
> Version: 0.2b3
>
> Type: Shareware
>
> Cost: $13.95

DBFax enables you to connect your PalmPilot to a fax-capable modem and send faxes. The fax is built from a MemoPad memo or from the Clipboard. DBFax is integrated into, the AddressBook application, allowing for easy look-up of the destinations fax number, and works with the PalmPilot clip-on modem and many others, which are listed at the Web site.

Net News

> Author: Gavin Peacock
>
> URL: None Given
>
> Version: 0.1a
>
> Type: Freeware
>
> Cost: N/A

Net News, as of this writing, is the one and only newsgroup reader application for the PalmPilot Professional. Like TG Postman and HandStamp Pro, Net News uses the built-in TCP/IP stack of the Professional model of PalmPilot, and does not run on any other model.

Though sparse in features, Net News proved that newsgroups (and TCP/IP applications) could be written for the PalmPilot, opening the door for others. Hopefully, by the time you read this, Net News will have been updated, or other newsgroup reader applications will have been released.

Online

Author: Iain Barclay
URL: http://www.hausofmaus.com
Version: 0.45
Type: Shareware
Cost: $20.00

Online is a VT-100 terminal emulator for the PalmPilot that allows you to connect to services at a full 80 characters (scrollable by using the hardware buttons) and 24 lines. By using Online and a shell account, you can read mail (via elm), read newsgroups (via tin), and even surf the Internet (via lynx). Of course, each of these applications must be available to your shell session. For those who would like a little-bitty VT-100 terminal, Online is the way to go!

Palmscape

**On the
CD-ROM**

Author: Kazuho Oku
URL: http://sodan.komaba.ecc.u-tokyo.ac.jp/~kazuho/
Version: PR4
Type: Freeware
Cost: N/A

Palmscape is a Web browser for the PalmPilot. Using the built-in TCP/IP support of the PalmPilot Pro (which means this app can't be run by non-Professional PalmPilots). Palmscape allows you to connect to the Web and browse your favorite sites. You can also define a cache, which allows you to first browse pages stored there, even if you're not connected. For now, however, you do have to first browse those pages while you are connected.

Palmscape, even in this early version, does an excellent job of displaying Web pages, and the author promises that it will improve. By the time you read this, I expect no fewer than three Web browsers to be available for the PalmPilot. I also anticipate other Web offerings, such as FTP and perhaps even IRC.

Top Gun Postman

On the CD-ROM

Author: Ian Goldberg and Steve Gribble

URL: http://www.isaac.cs.berkeley.edu/pilot/

Version: 1.2b

Type: Freeware

Cost: N/A

Top Gun Postman uses the PalmPilot Professional's built-in TCP/IP stack and e-mail applications to enable e-mail capability with the PalmPilot. You compose messages in the Mail app, go to TG Postman and select the **Send Mail** button (after you've configured the SMTP and POP preferences for your ISP) to send them. You select **Both** to send and receive mail.

Because Top Gun uses Professional-only applications/abilities, it cannot be used on a PalmPilot Personal or OS 1.x unit. If you have one of those units and need the capability to send and receive e-mail directly to and from the PalmPilot, your only option is the commercially available HandStamp (discussed in Chapter 5, "Commercial Software").

Top Gun Telnet

**On the
CD-ROM**

Author: Ian Goldberg
URL: http://www.isaac.cs.berkeley.edu/pilot/tgtelnet.html
Version: 1.0.0
Type: Freeware
Cost: N/A

Top Gun Telnet brings Telnet capability to your PalmPilot Professional. Like Top Gun Postman, TG Telnet uses (and requires) the built-in TCP/IP stack of the PalmPilot Professional, and therefore doesn't run on any other model.

World Finder

Author: Yamada Tatsushi
URL: http://www.tt.rim.or.jp/~tatsushi/indexe.html
Version: 0.2
Type: Freeware
Cost: N/A

World Finder was the first text-based Web browser for the PalmPilot. By the time you read this, there should be several others available (such as the Palmscape application, previously listed). PalmPilot browsers will never be anything fancy, but they do enable text Web browsing. Future versions will no doubt enable you to tap on a link to a .prc file and have that file installed on your PalmPilot.

Database

JFile

**On the
CD-ROM**

Author: John J. Lehett

URL: http://www.shoppersmart.com/jlehett/pilprogs.html

Version: 1.6b

Type: Shareware

Cost: $15.00

JFile is a simple generic database application with which you can create an unlimited number (although the shareware version limits you to two) of databases containing up to 20 fields each. In version 1.6b these are text fields, but the upcoming release of JFile (2.0, which should be out by the time you read this book) will add number, Boolean, and pop-up field types. Jfile enables the addition and deletion of fields on the fly (as will 2.0).

After you've created your database, you can specify those fields you'd like displayed on the record list screen. You can also filter records using specific criteria, search for text in any field, and quickly jump to a specific record number or to the bottom/top of the list.

Data can be entered either into the PalmPilot manually, or you can convert a comma-delimited text file to JFile format by using the supplied conversion program. This means you can quickly and easily transfer your data (or a subset of your data) to the PalmPilot for quick reference. This is a highly recommended app.

Figure 6.8 Record edit screen of JFile.

MED

On the CD-ROM

Author: Rick Bram

URL: http://www.palmglyph.com

Version: 0.61

Type: Freeware

Cost: N/A

Multiuser Editable Database, or MED, is a customizable version of the built-in AddressBook application, with a twist. MED allows two levels in each record. The top level is essentially equivalent to the AddressBook application, except that you can modify the field names, and each field can be defined as a pop-up with its own separate list of values. The second level allows you to attach as many records as you want to each first-level record, again with the ability to change any and all of the field names and define them as pop-up lists.

I was confused when I first read about this two-level approach, and the best way to understand the process is to install the application and play with it. To get to the second level of records, tap the **Down** button when you are browsing the top-level records.

As is, MED is a perfect solution for those who are looking for a configurable AddressBook application, and who are willing to make the extra effort to back up their data (MED supports import/export to and from the AddressBook application).

Simpledb

**On the
CD-ROM**

Author: Cassidy Lackey

URL: http://www.mobilegeneration.com

Version: v.41

Type: Shareware

Cost: $10.00

Using Simpledb, the user can create up to 10 custom databases. Records can include a heading and five fields; in addition, an unlimited number of free-form notes may be attached to each record. (Note: The unregistered version allows for a maximum of only five records per database.)

Desktop

Copilot

Author: Heath Hunnicutt

URL: http://ofb.net/~heath/pilot/copilot/

Version: 1.0b16

Type: Freeware

Cost: N/A

Taking the source code for Copilot (written by Greg Hewgill; see next entry), Heath Hunnicutt has added such features as PalmOS 2.0 and grayscale support. As with the original Copilot, in this version, you can view the PalmPilot as a black-and-white plain version or as a more realistic-looking PalmPilot. Missing from this version is backlighting, which is nice to have in realistic mode.

Figure 6.9 This version of Copilot supports grayscale rendering.

Copilot (Windows version)

> Author: Greg Hewgill
> URL: http://userzweb.lightspeed.net/~gregh
> Version: 1.0b8
> Type: Freeware
> Cost: N/A

Copilot is the Windows PalmPilot emulator. Using an extracted ROM file (the application to extract this ROM file is included with Copilot), you can emulate the PalmPilot on your desktop. For developers, Copilot comes in handy for testing applications. It is also a nice program to have when you want to try out a beta release, but don't want to risk your real PalmPilot. (Note: Copilot was instrumental in capturing the screenshots used throughout this book.)

Copilot (Mac version)

On the CD-ROM

> Author: C.B. Schofield
> URL: http://members.aol.com/illumesoft/copilot.html
> Version: 1.3
> Type: Freeware
> Cost: N/A

Copilot for the Macintosh was originally written for Windows by Greg Hewgill (see previous entry). It has become the de facto debugging tool used by developers to test their applications before moving them to a real PalmPilot.

DateBook to CSV Converter

Author: Ralph Griesenbeck

URL: http://www.inch.com/~ralphg/pilot/

Version: 0.4

Type: Freeware

Cost: N/A

This application allows you to convert the DateBook data file to a comma-delimited text file. You can then take the text file and import it to an Excel spreadsheet. This is a very useful capability, because currently, the PalmPilot Desktop software has no way to export DateBook records to this format (it only supports backing them up).

Fix PDB Dates

**On the
CD-ROM**

Author: Rusty Kay

URL: http://www.geocities.com/Eureka/1943/fixpdbdate.html

Version: 1.1

Type: Freeware

Cost: N/A

When the Pilot Desktop 1.0 for the Mac backs up .pdb files, the backup conduit changes the modification and creation dates to invalid values. This would not be a problem except that the install conduit refuses to install .pdb files with invalid dates. To the rescue comes Fix PDB Dates, a drag-and-drop AppleScript program that changes the creation and modification dates/times of a file (or files) that are dragged on top of it. Those files can then be reinstalled in your PalmPilot.

3Com recently released an update to the Mac Conduit Manager that should fix this problem, The fix is located at **http://www.3com.com/palm/custsupp/macconmgr.html.**

GCM

> Author: Pat Beirne
>
> URL: http://cpu563.adsl.sympatico.ca/gcm.htm
>
> Version: 0.23
>
> Type: Freeware
>
> Cost: N/A

General Conduit Manager, (or GCM), is a utility application in which you can define generic conduits that will sync to and from your PalmPilot. GCM provides data backup services for any PalmPilot app; fixes the data backup conduit problems of HotSync 1.0 or HotSync 1.1; enables easy selection of data-restore options; includes the update to DinkyView; speeds up the HotSync process; includes preconfigured setups for conduits (Dinky Pad, cbasPad, Pilot Money, PAL, and Jfile); and comes bundled with PC viewers for Dinky Pad, JFile, and cbasPad.

The latest version of GCM (GCM23/24) lets you build a complete backup of your PalmPilot, including all apps and data. This capability, which is integrated with RipCord, provides easy reinstallation of all data and applications in the event that a complete reinstall is necessary.

Graffiti Font

> Author: Stanley McKinley
>
> URL: http://homepages.together.net/~vtstan/
>
> Version: 1.0
>
> Type: Freeware
>
> Cost: N/A

Graffiti Font is a TrueType font of the Graffiti alphabet.

MakeDoc (DOS)

> Author: Pat Beirne
> URL: http://cpu563.adsl.sympatico.ca/default.htm
> Version: 0.8
> Type: Freeware
> Cost: N/A

MakeDoc is the DOS utility for converting text files to and from a .pdb format, which can be loaded into your PalmPilot for viewing with the Doc application. (This version can convert from the .pdb file to text.)

MakeDoc for Windows

> Author: Mark Pierce
> URL: http://ourworld.compuserve.com/homepages/Mark_Pierce/
> Version: 0.7
> Type: Freeware
> Cost: N/A

MakeDoc for Windows is the Win95 version of MakeDoc, which is used to convert text files to a format that can be loaded into your PalmPilot and read by the Doc application. MakeDoc for Windows supports many features, such as category support, automatic installation of converted files, and full control over line breaks. MakeDoc for Windows also supports section splitting, which allows you to create multiple Doc files for a large document. This is a nice feature for anyone with low memory, because you can load, read, and then delete one section at a time.

MakeDoc for Windows is the conversion program that I use, and I highly recommend it. The only thing it currently doesn't do that I wish it did (especially with DocPlus coming out) is convert from a .pdb file to a text file. Reportedly, however, this feature will have been added by the time you read this.

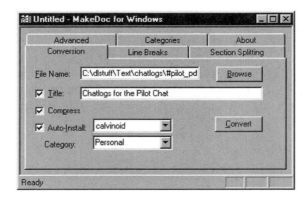

Figure 6.10 Conversion tab of the MakeDoc for Windows application.

MakeDocDD (Macintosh)

Author: Masatoshi Yoshizawa

URL: http://www.pluto.dti.ne.jp/~yoz/soft-e.html#MakeDocDD

Version: 1.0.2

Type: Freeware

Cost: N/A

MakeDocDD is the Mac application used to convert text files into Doc format, for use with Rick Bram's Doc or DocPlus reader application.

Pilot Address Selection Lib

**On the
CD-ROM**

Author: Joergen Pisarz

URL: http://ourworld.compuserve.com/homepages/pisarz

Version: 1.0

Type: Freeware

Cost: N/A

PilotADR.dll supports the selection and export of one address from the PalmPilot database without running the PalmPilot Desktop program. This utility is primarily for use with word processors, and comes with a Microsoft Word for Windows 6 and 7 macro and a Lotus Word Pro 96 script. These macros make buttons available in Word/Lotus Word Pro, which open a dialog showing the contents of the PalmPilot's address database.

Pilot Pal

**On the
CD-ROM**

Author: Precise Solutions

URL: http://www.precise-solutions.cix.co.uk/pilot.htm

Version: 2.00

Type: Shareware

Cost: $20.00

Pilot Pal provides a custom toolbar from which you can launch several PalmPilot-related functions. Pilot Pal keeps track of your favorite applications (it copies the files to a separate directory) so that you can reinstall them in one fell swoop if something causes a hard reset on the PalmPilot. Pilot Pal also allows you to specify favorite Web pages and applications to run from its toolbar; and you can click on a button to run the HotSync Manager or Desktop application.

Figure 6.11 Pilot Pal's toolbar.

PInstall

Author: Mark Pierce

URL: http://ourworld.compuserve.com/homepages/Mark_Pierce/

Version: 0.3

Type: Freeware

Cost: N/A

PInstall is a Windows 95/NT installation application that replaces the stock PalmPilot INSTAPP program. PInstall allows you to either double-click on a .prc file (running PInstall the first time sets up the proper associations) or use the Send To menu. Using PInstall, you can select multiple files to install; and using the Send To menu, you can install all of them at once. There are now several available alternate installation applications, but PInstall was one of the first, and is still one of the easiest to use. It is highly recommended.

Ripcord

Author: Harry Ohlsen
URL: http://wr.com.au/harryo/ripcord/
Version: 2.00
Type: Shareware
Cost: $10.00

Ripcord keeps track of the applications you have installed in your PalmPilot, and makes it easier to reinstall all of them in case you should need to do so. Ripcord also doubles as a PalmPilot application installer, allowing you to bypass using the PalmPilot INSTAPP application.

Web to Pilot

**On the
CD-ROM**

Author: Rusty Kay
URL: http://www.geocities.com/Eureka/1943/webtopilot.html
Version: 1.1
Type: Freeware
Cost: N/A

Web to Pilot is a Mac application that automates the process of downloading and converting to Doc for Web pages. Given a set of locations (URLs), Web to Pilot takes the pages, downloads and converts them (this requires separate applications), and then, using MakeDocDD, puts them in Doc format.

Finance

LoanCalc

On the
CD-ROM

Author: Jerry Wang

URL: http://www.directlogic.com

Version: 1.01

Type: Shareware

Cost: $10.00

LoanCalc is a simple application that calculates the monthly payment amount of a loan, given the initial loan amount, interest, and number of years. After quickly displaying the monthly amount, you are presented with an Amortize! button, which brings up a monthly amortization table for the specified loan. LoanCalc is a CASL application, and thus requires that the CASL runtime library be installed.

MoneyManager

Author: Jeremy Laurenson

URL: http://208.217.9.134/stinger/appinfo.cfm?ProgName=
    MoneyManager

Version: 1.64

Type: Freeware

Cost: N/A

Previously called PilotMoney, MoneyManager helps you keep track of your finances while on the go. Possibly the most popular application available for the PalmPilot, MoneyManager maintains all aspects of financial transactions for up to 16 different accounts. Descriptions and types can be predefined; and MoneyManager keeps a running balance for each account and informs you when that balance will be below zero. The application's options are too numerous to list, but suffice it to say that it has most of the essential features you would find in a desktop finance program.

Starting with version 1.64, MoneyManager will work only on OS 2.0 or higher. The 1.64 archive does contain, however, the 1.63 OS 1.0 release.

QMate

On the CD-ROM

Author: Steve Dakin

URL: http://www.wco.com/~sdakin/qmate.html

Version: 1.3.1

Type: Shareware

Cost: $15.00

With QMate, you can enter Quicken-specific financial information on your PalmPilot, and through the use of its accompanying conduit, generate .qif files, which can be imported into Quicken. Its features include the capability to synchronize data (supports categories, transactions, and memorized transactions) from your PalmPilot to Quicken on your PC or Mac via .qif files, QuickFill support for Payee and Category fields, memorized transactions, account transfers, up to 15 accounts (bank, cash, or credit card), flexible sorting and display options for showing only the transactions you want to see, auto-increment and decrement shortcuts for date and number fields, and support for the PalmPilot Expense application (including the Mac conduit).

Figure 6.12 The QuickFill feature of QMake automatically fills in fields for you, based on previously memorized transactions.

QuickTip

Author: Brad Cleveland

URL: http://www.ablecom.net/~brad/

Version: 1.0

Type: Shareware

Cost: $7.00

Using QuickTip, you enter a food bill (total, tax, and tip percentage) and calculates the total tip amount. QuickTip also lets you specify the number of it people in the party, and divides the total tip amount by that number.

TipMaster

Author: Andy Sackheim

URL: http://www.ascii.net/tip.htm

Version: 1.1

Type: Shareware

Cost: $8.00

TipMaster is a simple little application that enables you to quickly calculate the tip for any service requiring a gratuity. You enter the tip percentage and the amount of the check, and TipMaster returns the correct tip and total bill amount.

Games

4 In Line

On the CD-ROM

Author: Tan Kok Mun

URL: http://home.pacific.net.sg/~kokmun/basic.htm

Version: 1.5

Type: Shareware

Cost: $15.00

The 4 In Line game is a Connect 4 port for the PalmPilot. Features include a 3-D look, real-time indicator of the PalmPilot's thought process, and full undo ability. The computer player can be set to different skill levels; at the upper levels it is quite good. This game will beat you very easily, even at the lower levels, if you're not paying attention. It's great fun!

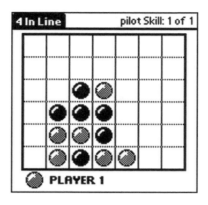

Figure 6.13 Tan Kok Mun's 4 In Line game.

Ataxx

On the CD-ROM

Author: Valavan Manohararajah

URL: http://www.pilotgear.com

Version: 1.0

Type: Freeware

Cost: N/A

Ataxx is a board game in which your goal is to end up with the most pieces in your color when all the squares are filled in. At each turn, you must move an existing piece one square or two. Moving a piece one square leaves the original piece, while duplicating it in the selected square; moving a piece two squares actually moves that piece. Once placed, all pieces of the opposite color that touch the selected square are flipped. It sounds simple, but after playing a game or two and ending up with only a smattering of pieces, you'll soon realize that there is a strategy to this game!

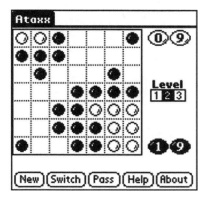

Figure 6.14 I'm playing white and getting beat.

Black Box

On the CD-ROM

Author: Matt Peterson

URL: http://www.dovcom.com

Version: 1.01

Type: Shareware

Cost: $10.00

Black Box consists of a grid of 8x8 squares. Under the squares, balls are hiding (the number of balls is up to you). To locate the balls, you fire laser beams, then decipher the various resulting symbols that appear around the outside of the box. It's an interesting and very challenging game.

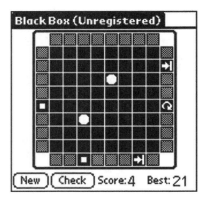

Figure 6.15 Black Box.

Blackjack

**On the
CD-ROM**

Author: RedTail Software

URL: http://www.redtailsoft.com

Version: 1.0

Type: Shareware

Cost: $14.00

Blackjack is a standard two-player game of cards, with some nice features, including the ability to specify a table limit, configure the number of decks and play speed, and much more. This is a very good rendition of blackjack, so if you enjoy this game, this version or "implementation" will keep you busy for hours. (Note that the unregistered shareware version included on the CD expires 15 days after you first run it.)

Figure 6.16 BlackJack by RedTail Software.

Blackout

On the
CD-ROM

Author: Jeff Jetton

URL: http://www.mindspring.com/~jetton/pilot/index.html

Version: 1.0

Type: Shareware

Cost: $7.00

Blackout is one of my favorite games for the PalmPilot. The premise is simple: You press a square to toggle that and all surrounding squares to the other color. The object is to turn all of the squares to black. There are 35 preset levels, and you can randomly generate other levels (you specify in how many steps the level can be solved). Registered users that make it to the end of the 35 preset levels will be given a code phrase that can be e-mailed to the author, to be recognized on his Blackout Hall of Fame Web page (so far, three people have accomplished this—and I was the first!).

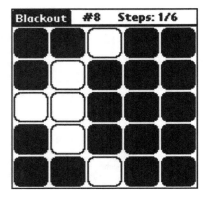

Figure 6.17 Level 6, still fairly easy.

Block Party

Author: Chuck Jordan

URL: http://www.mindspring.com/~torgo/pilot/index.html

Version: 1.0

Type: Freeware

Cost: N/A

Block Party is one of the better Tetris-like games for the PalmPilot. You control the blocks with the hardware buttons (spin, move left/right, and drop). The blocks look a little nicer than some of the other Tetris games available, and play starts out nice and slow to let you get the hang of things. When a line disappears, the little explosion animation is a nice touch. All in all, it's a good game.

Figure 6.18 Block Party is a good Tetris game for the PalmPilot.

Blocks

**On the
CD-ROM**

Author: Bill Kirby

URL: http://electronhut.com/pilot/

Version: 1.0

Type: Freeware

Cost: N/A

Blocks is a simple Tetris clone. You use the four hardware buttons to move and spin the blocks. Warning: Blocks tends to run a tad fast on machines that have over 512 K.

Crossbow

Author: Harry Ohlsen
URL: http://wr.com.au/harryo/crossbow
Version: 1.03
Type: Shareware
Cost: $5.00

Crossbow is a crossword puzzle application that takes specially formatted memos (stored in a Crosswords category in MemoPad) with which you solve the puzzle. A large number of puzzles are available to choose from; or you can convert *USA Today* and *New York Times* puzzles with one of the available conversion programs.

Emerald Hunt

On the
CD-ROM

Author: Scott Powell
URL: http://www.kagi.com/scottpowell/
Version: 1.2
Type: Shareware
Cost: $7.00

This is an action game similar to the classic Boulderdash. With four-way scrolling, and using pen input to control the play, your goal is to dig through dirt, collecting gems, while avoiding being crushed by boulders, blown up, or drowned. You can also design your own levels using a simple Win95 program to create level databases.

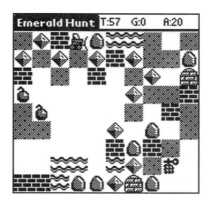

Figure 6.19 Beginning of a level in Emerald Hunt.

FlipIt

**On the
CD-ROM**

Author: Matt Peterson

URL: http://www.dovcom.com

Version: 1.1

Type: Shareware

Cost: $5.00

Similar to Jeff Jetton's Blackout, FlipIt is similar to the popular hand-held game Lights Out, where the object is to turn off all the lights, starting with a predetermined (or random) pattern. FlipIt was the first of this type of game released for the PalmPilot, and needs to be updated to add some of the features of Blackout. However, FlipIt is a couple of bucks cheaper, and is the same basic game, which is very enjoyable.

Fore!

**On the
CD-ROM**

Author: Frank MacBride

URL: http://macbride.com/~macbride/pilot/

Version: 1.0

Type: Shareware

Cost: $5.00

Fore! is based on a golf dice game, in which you roll a set of dice that determines your score for each hole; then you pass the dice to the next player. Fore! duplicates this game somewhat, although the dice are buttons on the PalmPilot screen (they don't resemble dice). It's a fun game, but I'd like to see more options, such as a true single-player mode, best scores/rounds, and so on. Fore! was written using CASL, which means it requires the CASL runtime module to operate.

FreeCell

**On the
CD-ROM**

Author: Bill Kirby

URL: http://www.electronhut.com/pilot/

Version: 1.0

Type: Shareware

Cost: $12.00

FreeCell is a game of solitaire, written by the man that brought Klondike solitaire to the PalmPilot. If you've played Klondike, you'll recognize the similarities in interface and design, and appreciate the completeness with which Bill Kirby implements the game of FreeCell. If you enjoy a good game of solitaire, and are tired of playing Klondike, give FreeCell a try.

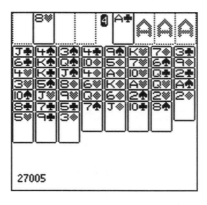

Figure 6.20 FreeCell from Bill Kirby.

Gem Hunt

Author: Jeff Jetton
URL: http://www.mindspring.com/~jetton/pilot/index.html
Version: 1.0
Type: Shareware
Cost: $7.00

Gem Hunt is a puzzle/logic game, in which you try to determine the location of hidden gems based on the entry and exit points of selectable laser beams. Given the number of times you fire, and whether you've correctly (or incorrectly) guessed the location of the hidden gems, you are given a score. My advice: Peruse the included Read Me file very carefully, as Jetton gives an extensive explanation of Beam Movement 101, revealing how the beams are affected by gem placement. Gem Hunt is a great game for logic puzzle lovers.

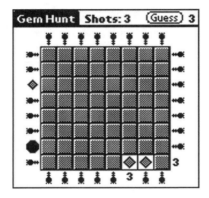

Figure 6.21 Gem Hunt by Jeff Jetton.

Golf Solitaire

**On the
CD-ROM**

Author: Jeff Jetton
URL: http://www.mindspring.com/~jetton/pilot/index.html

Version: 1.1

Type: Shareware

Cost: $8.00

Golf Solitaire has always been one of my favorite time-wasting activities. The only thing I never liked to do was set up the cards. Now, with my PalmPilot and Golf Solitaire, I can play a game without bringing along a deck. This game is also available in the Patience application (covered later in this section), but this version looks better, and includes such niceties as a LeaderBoard (Hi Score table), and the option to start where you left off in the last game. My best score so far? -3.

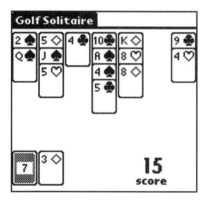

Figure 6.22 Golf Solitaire, a great game by Jeff Jetton.

Guess Me

**On the
CD-ROM**

Author: Tan Kok Mun
URL: http://home1.pacific.net.sg/~kokmun/pilotpgm.htm
Version: 1.5
Type: Shareware
Cost: $12.00

If you know how to play MasterMind, then you know the premise behind Guess Me: You try to figure out what the hidden symbols are. (The symbols can be configured as numbers or patterns.) To play, you insert guesses in the box provided, then tap on the **OK** button. In response, you are told how many symbols you guessed correctly, and how many you guessed correctly but in a wrong position. Using these visual clues, you continue to guess at the hidden pattern until you get it right. The screen flashes when you have succeeded. At any point, you can ask for a hint or begin a new game.

Guess Me enhances the MasterMind scheme by allowing you to configure code size, the number of possible symbols/numbers/patterns, and the maximum allowable duplicates. These options and the well-written interface provide anyone who enjoys logic games with enough variations to ward off monotony.

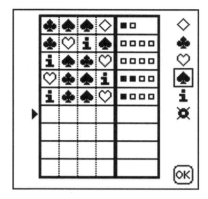

Figure 6.23 Guess Me is like the old MasterMind game.

Hangman

**On the
CD-ROM**

Author: David Haupert

URL: http://www.gate.net/~dhaupert/ddhpilot.html

Version: 1.0

Type: Shareware

Cost: $12.00

In this version of Hangman for the PalmPilot, you can play with either one or two. The interface is simple: You click on a letter to guess that letter, which then appears in the proper place in the puzzle, or you add another body part to the noose. Other features include a hint option, puzzle categories, and the option to give up before swinging. The shareware version comes with 35 puzzles; the registered version comes with multiple databases that can be added/removed individually (for potentially thousands of puzzles) and eliminates the annoying splash screen.

Hit!

On the
CD-ROM

> Author: Frank MacBride
> URL: http://macbride.com/~macbride/pilot/
> Version: 1.0
> Type: Donorware
> Cost: $5.00

The object of Hit! is to guess which of three hidden buttons has the lowest number underneath it. You are given 20 tries, and the highest number of hits is recorded as the High Score. Hit! requires the CASL runtime module to run.

HMaki

**On the
CD-ROM**

Author: Holger Klawitter

URL: http://wwwmath.uni-muenster.de/math/inst/info/u/ holger/
pilot/hmaki.html

Version: 1.7

Type: Postcardware

Cost: Postcard

HMaki is an interesting game of patterns. The object of the game is to
select blocks of the same pattern to form an area; a second tap removes that
area. The larger the area and the higher percentage of the remaining blocks,
the higher the score for removing those blocks. Sound easy? The game itself
is easy, but achieving a high score, especially if you're playing with several
patterns (you can specify the number of patterns to use, as well as a grid
size), is a different story. HMaki is one of those games you'll start playing,
and over an hour later, wonder where the time went.

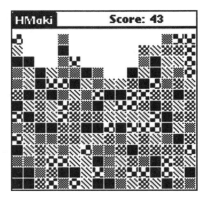

Figure 6.24 HMaki is addictive.

inComing

On the
CD-ROM

Author: Tan Kok Mun

URL: http://home.pacific.net.sg/~kokmun/basic.htm

Version: 1.2

Type: Shareware

Cost: $12.00

inComing is one of two currently available Missile Command-like games for the PalmPilot. The other one (MissileCmd) mimics the arcade game more closely, but inComing offers some enhancements that make it more of a challenge. For instance, the number of missiles is almost always less than the total number of incoming missiles, so you must time your shots to take out more than one each time. Add to this the variations such as an arsenal of incoming weapons, day and night mode, and other user-selectable options, and you've got a game that is both true to the original and different enough to make it a challenge.

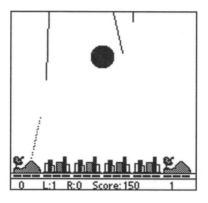

Figure 6.25 Missiles are at a premium in inComing.

Jookerie

Author: John J. Lehett
URL: http://www.shoppersmart.com/jlehett/pilprogs.html
Version: 1.0
Type: Shareware
Cost: $12.00

Jookerie players start by choosing an unfamiliar word, make up their own definitions, and each player tries to guess which is the correct definition.

My main complaint with Jookerie is that it doesn't really play well on the platform, as it requires players to enter (using Graffiti) each definition for each round. After a few rounds, many people will reach for paper and pencil to enjoy the original version.

JT WOF

On the CD-ROM

> Author: Scott Duensing
> URL: http://www.jaegertech.com
> Version: 1.20
> Type: Freeware
> Cost: N/A

JT WOF is a three-player Wheel of Fortune game for the PalmPilot. The graphics are similar to those used on the television version. There's even a separate graphics file containing Pat and Vanna images. You can also add more puzzles (Puzzle Pack is included on the CD) and various other graphics to modify the game. Letters are entered using Graffiti, so you can get in a little Graffiti practice while you play.

Klondike

On the CD-ROM

> Author: Bill Kirby
> URL: http://www.electronhut.com/pilot/
> Version: 1.3

Type: Shareware

Cost: $12.00

Klondike is arguably the most popular computer game ever written, so it's no surprise that it's one of the most popular games for the PalmPilot. The application has the standard options, along with Vegas rules, selectable number of decks (one or three), and several interface options.

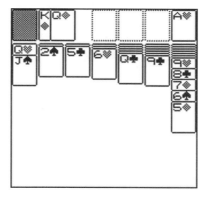

Figure 6.26 Klondike solitaire for your PalmPilot.

LetItRide

On the CD-ROM

Author: Ron Gouldner

URL: http://www.exit109.com/~ron/pilot

Version: 2.0

Type: Shareware

Cost: $11.95

LetItRide is a gambling game popular in Las Vegas, Atlantic City, and other casino venues. It is a stud poker-style game in which you either take back part of your bet or let it ride. Perhaps by playing the game on your PalmPilot, you can learn a few tricks, then win a few extra dollars the next time you play it for real. To that end, LetItRide has a mode in which you are warned when you are not playing according to the optimal strategy.

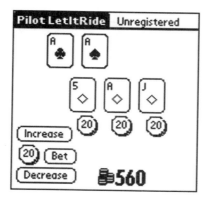

Figure 6.27 LetItRide brings the game straight from the casino to your PalmPilot.

Match

Author: Alex Garza

URL: http://www.giga.com/~agarza/pilot/match/

Version: 1.4

Type: Shareware

Cost: $5.00

Match is a concentration game: Hidden under 30 squares are a mix and match of several different icons. When you select two icons that match, two cards are removed. The goal is to remove all of the cards on the board. Match is highly recommended for youngsters.

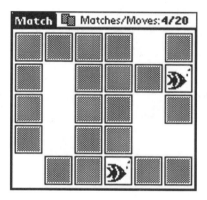

Figure 6.28 Good—a match!

Mind Meld

On the
CD-ROM

      Author: Ron Gouldner

      URL: http://www.exit109.com/~ron/pilot/

      Version: 2.0

      Type: Shareware

      Cost: $11.95

Mind Meld is a game in which you try to guess a series of letters chosen by your PalmPilot. The application maintains statistics for games played, and has settings to make the games easier or more difficult; it also provides the basic interface to play a game of MasterMind.

MissileCmd

On the CD-ROM

Author: Jesse Donaldson

URL: http://conrtrib.andrew.cmu.edu/usr/galahad/

Version: 1.01

Type: Freeware

Cost: N/A

MissileCmd is a rendition of the classic arcade game, miniaturized to fit on your PalmPilot. Missiles are directed by tapping their destination on the screen, and are dispatched from the closest city with a missile left. MissileCmd more closely resembles its arcade predecessor than the shareware application inComing. For instance, the exploding missiles can cause other missiles to explode when hit. It also starts out at a quicker pace than inComing.

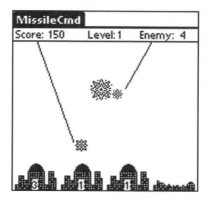

Figure 6.29 Missile Command for your PalmPilot.

Patience

Author: Keith Packard

URL: http://www.reed.edu/~keith/pilot/pilot.html

Version: 2.3

Type: Freeware

Cost: N/A

Patience is a collection of freeware solitaire card games bundled in one application: Aces High, Calculation, Golf, Klondike, Montana, Spider, Spiderette, Tabby Cat, Towers, and Yukon. Patience doesn't have any of the bells and whistles of the dedicated solitaire games, but basic game play works just fine.

Pegged

On the
CD-ROM

Author: Tan Kok Mun

URL: http://home1.pacific.net.sg/~kokmun/pilotpgm.htm

Version: 2.0

Type: Shareware

Cost: $12.00

Pegged re-creates the old wooden pegboard games where you had to jump over pegs to remove them, with the object being to remove all but one peg. Pegged comes with several built-in boards and initial peg configurations; or you can choose to randomly build a configuration.

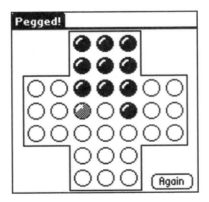

Figure 6.30 Leave just one peg to win.

Perplex

**On the
CD-ROM**

Author: Matt Peterson

URL: http://www.dovcom.com

Version: 1.0

Type: Shareware

Cost: $6.00

Perplex is a sliding block puzzle game. The object is to slide the pieces around so that you can maneuver the large square block, that starts at the top of the screen, to the bottom of the screen.

Pikoban

**On the
CD-ROM**

Author: Tan Kok Mun

URL: http://home.pacific.net.sg/~kokmun/pilotpgm.htm

Version: 1.5

Type: Shareware

Cost: $12.00

Pikoban is a logic puzzle game in which players attempt to push the boxes onto the loading platform. Get one box stuck in a corner, and you will have to start the level over. The pusher is activated by tapping the screen at the location you want a box. Pikoban comes with 50 levels (registering makes you eligible for Pikoban-2, with 40 more levels), all playable in the shareware version. As with the other applications from Tan Kok Mun, you are given 30 games to determine whether you like the shareware, then experience an ever-increasing delay before the game will start.

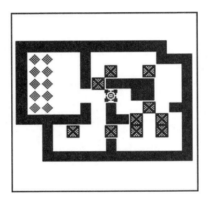

Figure 6.31 Move your boxes without getting them stuck.

PocketChess

Author: Scott Ludwig

URL: http://www.eskimo.com/~scottlu/pilot/

Version: 1.0

Type: Freeware

Cost: N/A

PocketChess enables you to play a game of chess on your PalmPilot. You can play another person or against the PalmPilot, which can be set to one of eight skill levels. To give you an idea how competitive play is, most average chess players report that they get beat more often than not on even the lower levels. I've only succeeded in beating level 1 once.

Figure 6.32 Chess on the PalmPilot? You bet!

PocketGammon

Author: Shuji Fukumoto

URL: http://www.wakuwaku.or.jp/shuji

Version: 1.2.5

Type: Shareware

Cost: $15.00

PocketGammon brings the exciting game of Backgammon to your PalmPilot. This version features all the popular aspects of the game, including use of the doubling cube and the ability to move a pip multiple squares for a given dice roll (for example, moving 11 spaces at once with a 5/6 roll). You can play against the PalmPilot or another person.

PocketGammon displays good graphics, and the PalmPilot's play seems to improve with each version.

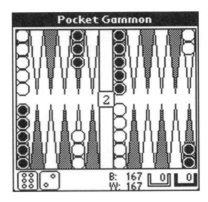

Figure 6.33 Opening screen for PocketGammon.

PV Poker

Author: Mike Therien

URL: http://web2.airmail.net/mike2me/Pilot/

Version: 1.2

Type: Freeware

Cost: N/A

This is a simple draw poker game for the PalmPilot, similar to many of the video poker machines that you see in casinos. Therien has stopped working on PV Poker to concentrate his efforts on Casino Poker, a much improved version of the same type of game (which should be available by the time you read this).

Pyramid

**On the
CD-ROM**

Author: James Lee

URL: http://www.engin.umd.umich.edu/~scubajl/ss/ss.html

Version: 1.0

Type: Freeware

Cost: N/A

This is the classic Pyramid solitaire game, brought to the PalmPilot. To play, you remove cards in pairs totaling 13 (kings may be removed singly). The game features a high-score list, as well as multiple-play levels (the easy level allows reshuffle, etc.). This is another good solitaire game for the PalmPilot.

Rally 1000

**On the
CD-ROM**

Author: David Mayes

URL: http://www.users.cts.com/crash/m/mayes/pilot.html

Version: 2.0

Type: Freeware

Cost: N/A

Rally 1000 is a very entertaining card game, whose object is to race against the computer player. This is accomplished by playing one of a multitude of mileage, remedy, and hazard cards. Rally 1000 takes some time to learn (full instructions are included), but once you have the hang of it, it is addictive. My only complaint is that the computer player always seems to get the good cards, making it very tough to win.

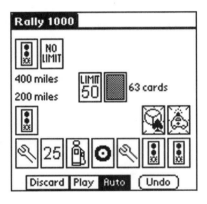

Figure 6.34 The Rally 1000 screen.

Reptoids

Author: Roger Flores

URL: None Given

Version: 1.8

Type: Freeware

Cost: N/A

Reptoids is the PalmPilot version of Asteroids. Using the hardware buttons to control your ship, you maneuver in and around asteroids, simultaneously blowing them to bits. Note that version 1.8 runs only on the new PalmPilot OS 2.0; version 1.0 is still running on older machines.

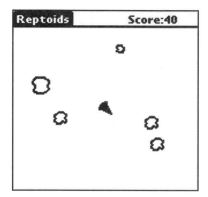

Figure 6.35 Reptoids brings a classic arcade game to the palm of your hand.

SingleNumber

**On the
CD-ROM**

Author: Yoshimitsu Kanai

URL: None Given

Version: 1.4

Type: Shareware

Cost: $10.00

SingleNumber presents the player with a 9x9 matrix, and each cell of this matrix contains another 9x9 matrix. The object of the game is to place the numbers 1 to 9 in such a way that each appears only once in the smaller 3x3 matrix, as well as only once in each row and column of the larger matrix.

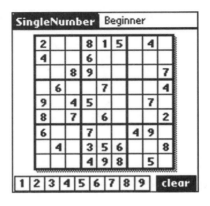

Figure 6.36 The start of a new SingleNumber game.

Slots

**On the
CD-ROM**

Author: Jerry Wang

URL: http://www.directlogic.com

Version: 1.0

Type: Shareware

Cost: $10.00

You guessed it, Slots is a simple slot machine game for the PalmPilot. Written in CASL, it requires the CASL runtime module (included in the .zip file) to operate.

Sokoban

On the CD-ROM

Author: Bill Kirby

URL: http://www.electronhut.com/pilot/

Version: 1.0

Type: Shareware

Cost: $12.00

Sokoban is another interesting puzzle game. The object is to push boxes around a maze to a specified location. It's not as easy as it sounds, because you can't pull a box, only push. And did I mention you can push only one box at a time? If you push a box into a corner or up against another box and you can't push in another direction, you're stuck!

To make moving a little easier, Sokoban uses something called Smart Move, which allows you to tap somewhere on the board and have your little man move there (or have him move a box there; this is configurable). Sokoban is a fun and challenging game (I haven't made it past level 2 of the 50 available) that any puzzle enthusiast will enjoy.

Space Invaders

Author: Scott Ludwig

URL: http://www.eskimo.com/~scottlu/pilot/

Version: 1

Type: Freeware

Cost: N/A

Here is another classic arcade game come to life on your PalmPilot. Space Invaders is a fairly good interpretation of the original: You move your ship and fire using the hardware buttons.

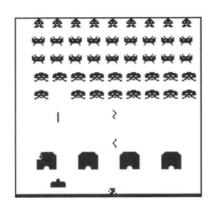

Figure 6.37 Space Invaders for the PalmPilot.

Ted-Truss

On the CD-ROM

Author: Tony Leung

URL: http://www.arcosoft.com

Version: 1.0

Type: Freeware

Cost: N/A

Ted-Truss is another Tetris-like game for the PalmPilot. Its capabilities include preview of next piece, change speed on the fly, optional landscape, play using Graffiti or real buttons, and small memory footprint.

TicTacToe

On the CD-ROM

Author: Frank MacBride

URL: http://www.macbride.com/~macbride/pilot/

Version: 1.0

Type: Shareware

Cost: $5.00

TicTacToe is a CASL application that allows two to play a game of TicTacToe. Each player taps the position to place his or her next move. When a game has been won, TicTacToe gives the option to play another game.

Wheel of Treasure

On the CD-ROM

Author: David Haupert

URL: http://www.gate.net/~dhaupert/ddhpilot.html

Version: 0.95

Type: Shareware

Cost: $12.00

Wheel of Treasure is another PalmPilot edition of Wheel of Fortune (without Vanna, though); you can spin the wheel, buy a vowel, and so on. The shareware version comes with 35 puzzles; the registered version gives you several more databases that can be installed/uninstalled for thousands of puzzles. Wheel of Treasure and Hangman (written by the same author) share the same puzzle databases, so they might start to look familiar. The big difference is that Hangman allows up to only two players, whereas Wheel allows up to 10. If you don't mind passing around your PalmPilot in a group of friends, Wheel of Treasure is a game you and your friends will enjoy.

Figure 6.38 Spin the wheel and guess the puzzle.

yahtChallenge

**On the
CD-ROM**

Author: Tan Kok Mun

URL: http://home.pacific.net.sg/~kokmun/pilotpgm.htm

Version: 1.8

Type: Shareware

Cost: $12.00

yahtChallenge brings the popular dice game to your PalmPilot. When you start a new game of yahtChallenge, you can choose to play against a computer opponent (with four varying risk factors), the number of rolls per turn, and the number of games to play in the match, or challenge. From there, the game follows the standard rules of the classic dice game: You are given the selected number of rolls to complete a set series of combinations. Once you have completed your rolls (or you decide the current throw was good enough to preclude rolling further), you select in which of the combinations to place your score. Running scores are kept for each player, and you can view the other player's scoresheet at any time.

yahtChallenge is a great game, one that I've had on my PalmPilot since it was released. If you like the classic dice game, you'll love being able to play it out of your pocket.

Figure 6.39 yahtChallenge, a great dice game by Tan Kok Mun.

ZIP

**On the
CD-ROM**

Author: Rick Bram

URL: http://www.palmglyph.com

Version: 1.25

Type: Shareware

Cost: $12.00

ZIP is a Z-Code Interpreter Program that runs text adventure games (after they're converted) such as those from Infocom. Its features include a pop-up menu of commonly used commands and the capability to tap on a word in the text to automatically place that word in the command line.

ZIP doesn't come with any games; they must be downloaded, and the best site for this is Leisa ReFalo's Interactive Fiction for the Pilot page (**http://www.geocities.com/Heartland/9590/interactive.htm**). ReFalo has not only compiled a list of games that work with ZIP, but she has converted them so that they're ready to load.

Graphics

Dinky Pad

On the CD-ROM

Author: Ed Keyes
URL: http://www.daggerware.com
Version: 0.92b
Type: Shareware
Cost: $5.00

Dinky Pad is a drawing/doodling application, one of the first available for the PalmPilot. While not as full-featured as newer competing graphics applications, Dinky Pad still offers a lot the others do not. The ability to quickly and smoothly scroll the canvas with the page up/down buttons makes Dinky Pad the best application for taking notes. And you can attach text notes to each drawing. The drawing list thumbnails are unique in that they show the text and the full size of a drawing, including a little window indicating where you were last viewing the image.

Dinky Pad drawings can be moved to and from the desktop (PC only) using the General Conduit Manager (GCM) by Pat Beirne. This application also comes with DinkyView, which allows you to view and manipulate your Dinky Pad drawings on the desktop. Hopefully, by the time you read this, Dinky Pad 1.x will have been released. Promising features such as grayscale support and flood fills, this release should put Dinky Pad back on top.

Figure 6.40 Dinky Pad drawing list screen.

Doodle

Author: Roger E. Critchlow Jr.

URL: http://www.elf.org/pilot/doodle.html

Version: 0.6

Type: Freeware

Cost: N/A

Doodle may be a small graphics application, but it doesn't scrimp on features. With it you can create multiple pages and flip through them using the up/down buttons. Along with the standard options to set pen size and draw/erase mode, Doodle includes a smear mode in which you can, well, smear portions of the drawing with the brush. If you're looking for a small, free graphics application, you need look no further than Doodle.

HDSketch

Author: Hitchhiker Design

URL: http://www.hhd.com/

Version: 1.1

Type: Shareware

Cost: $20.00

The HDSketch drawing application includes standard drawing tools such as line, box, circle, and freehand, and supports both horizontal and vertical scrolling. HDSketch comes with a PC conduit and application, so that you can import and export drawings to and from the PC (Windows 95/NT only).

PalmDraw

On the CD-ROM

Author: Brad Goodman

URL: http://www.oai.com/bkg/Pilot/

Version: 1.0b8

Type: Shareware

Cost: $10.00

PalmDraw is an object-based graphics tool for the PalmPilot that enables you to move, resize, and delete individual objects within a drawing. When you are done with your drawing, you can either print to a serial PostScript printer, or export the PostScript code to the MemoPad application.

Though perhaps not as easy to use as graphics-only applications such as TealPaint and Dinky Pad, PalmDraw excels when you need to be able to move objects around and to have access to features such as snap-to-grid and PostScript output.

Photo Album

Author: Mark Oberman

URL: http://members.aol.com/pilotphoto/

Version: 3.0

Type: Shareware

Cost: $15.00

Photo Album makes it possible to carry pictures in grayscale or high-contrast black and white on your PalmPilot. The view application is complemented by the Photo Album Studio program, which is the program that runs on the desktop and converts .bmp files to Photo Album format.

SketchPad

On the CD-ROM

Author: Tony Leung

URL: http://www.arcosoft.com

Version: 1.01

Type: Freeware

Cost: N/A

SketchPad is just what its name says it is, a simple sketch application. Each sketch can be copied and pasted to a new sketch, and the page up/down keys move you from sketch to sketch. These two features allow you to create rudimentary animations (pressing the page buttons flips through the frames). SketchPad does not have all the bells and whistles of other graphics applications, but it is a good freeware alternative.

TealPaint

**On the
CD-ROM**

Author: Vince Lee

URL: http://www.tealpoint.com

Version: 1.00

Type: Shareware

Cost: $17.95

TealPaint is a full-featured graphics and drawing application whose features include: record annotation capability, list view with thumbnail images, multiple drawing tools (freehand, line, box, circle, etc.), multiple modification tools (erase, paint/fill, text, selector), 16 draw/fill patterns, 12 brushes, and a screen-grabbing utility. An included conversion application lets you extract the images to the desktop from the backup file created during a HotSync. (Note: Desktop-to-PalmPilot conversion is not currently supported.)

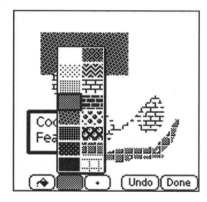

Figure 6.41 Examples of the fills available in TealPaint.

HackMaster Hacks

The applications, or hacks, mentioned in this section require the HackMaster application, which is discussed later in this chapter in the Utilities section.

AppHack

**On the
CD-ROM**

Author: Ed Keyes

URL: http://www.daggerware.com

Version: 1.01

Type: Shareware

Cost: $5.00

With AppHack, you can configure your hardware buttons to run any application currently installed on your PalmPilot. The new 2.0 OS capability to assign an application to a button is taken one step further by AppHack, which allows you to specify a two-button combination to run an application. When you press one of the four hardware application buttons, you are shown the list of buttons to which you've assigned applications. Therefore, you can assign six applications to each of the four hardware buttons (you can use the page up/down buttons for the second button press).

Using the AppHack configuration screen shown in Figure 6.41, you would press the **To Do** button, then the **AddressBook** button to run the CurrCalc application. To assign one application to a button, thereby bypassing the submenu, you would simply assign all of the buttons to that application. The configuration screen enables you to do this easily by setting the top button to the application desired, and selecting the **Set all to top** button.

Figure 6.42 Configuring AppHack.

BackHack

**On the
CD-ROM**

Author: Jeff Jetton

URL: http://www.mindspring.com/~jetton/pilot/index.html

Version: 1.0

Type: Freeware

Cost: N/A

A nifty little hack, BackHack reverses all the text on your PalmPilot, including the menus and system dialogs. Obviously, this is not a very useful application, but it is good for a laugh or two.

Figure 6.43 BackHacked standard Address Edit screen.

BatteryHack

Author: Matt Peterson

URL: http://www.dovcom.com/pilot/batthack.html

Version: 1.01

Type: Freeware

Cost: N/A

BatteryHack changes the battery voltage meter in the built-in application picker from a bar to a number, representing the current battery volts. This is a good hack to have if you don't use PAL or Launchpad, as seeing the actual voltage gives you a better indication of how your batteries are doing. Note: BatteryHack does not work with the new PalmPilot OS 2.0 or higher. If you have a PalmPilot (or have upgraded your 1000/5000 to OS 2.0), do not load this hack.

CalcHack

Author: Matt Peterson

URL: http://www.dovcom.com

Version: 2.1

Type: Freeware

Cost: N/A

When you tap the **Calculator** silkscreen button, CalcHack lets you select from a list of eight shareware/freeware calculators. Note that this hack is no longer necessary with OS 2.0, on which you can define any application by tapping the **Calculator** button. Also, because the calculator applications are hard-coded, more recent calculators do not show up in the list.

ClipHack

On the
CD-ROM

Author: Murray Dowling

URL: http://www.icms.com.au/pilot/

Version: 1.0

Type: Shareware

Cost: $7.00

Using ClipHack, you can cut and paste any size text block to and from PalmPilot applications. The standard Clipboard allows for only a certain size (which never seems large enough). When you cut the text, ClipHack also displays the number of words and characters in a nice little pop-up box that stays on the screen for a couple of seconds (and can be dismissed more quickly by tapping it).

ClipHack is an application that should have been included in PalmOS (like FindHack). I highly recommend it.

FindHack

Author: Florent Pillet

URL: http://w3.teaser.fr/~fpillet/pilot/

Version: 1.0

Type: Freeware

Cost: N/A

PalmPilot's built-in Find feature doesn't allow you to search for text in the middle of a word. For instance, searching for town would find Townplace but not Allentown. FindHack allows you to find text regardless of where in a word it is located. I highly recommend FindHack to every PalmPilot owner.

HushHack

On the
CD-ROM

Author: Jeff Jetton

URL: http://www.mindspring.com/~jetton/pilot/index.html

Version: 1

Type: Freeware

Cost: N/A

HushHack is a simple program that turns off the HotSync sounds. If you have PalmOS 2.0 and have the System sound option in Prefs turned off, you don't need this hack, but if you have OS 1.0 and don't like the HotSync tones, you'll appreciate HushHack.

MenuHack

On the CD-ROM

Author: Ed Keyes

URL: http://www.daggerware.com

Version: 1.2

Type: Freeware

Cost: N/A

MenuHack allows you to access an application's menu by pressing the Title bar of the application (if displayed), rather than pressing the silkscreen Menu button.

PowerHack

Author: Jack Russell

URL: http://dspace.dial.pipex.com/jakr/pilot/

Version: 0.93

Type: Freeware

Cost: N/A

PowerHack is used to automatically lock the PalmPilot when it has been turned off. It is also required by the Check-In application, in order to display the Check-In screen at powerup.

SelectHack

On the
CD-ROM

Author: Jeff Jetton

URL: http://www.mindspring.com/~jetton/pilot/index.html

Version: 1.0

Type: Shareware

Cost: $5.00

Using SelectHack you can, in any PalmPilot application, double-tap on a word to highlight that word; you can also triple-tap to select an entire paragraph. Preferences options include SmartSelect (which adds adjacent spaces to allow easy word deletion) and tap speed alternatives. SelectHack should have been implemented in PalmOS to start with, and along with FindHack and ClipHack, are the must-have hacks.

SwitchHack

On the
CD-ROM

Author: Murray Dowling

URL: http://www.icms.com.au/pilot/

Version: 1.0

Type: Shareware

Cost: $5.00

SwitchHack lets you quickly switch back from the application you are currently in to the one you were in previously. Suppose, for example, you're playing a game of Klondike, and someone asks you about the current state of a project you're working on. You flip to Launchpad, select **Outliner**, give that person the information, and then use SwitchHack to quickly return to your game. SwitchHack has built-in support for many built-in and third-party applications. I highly recommend SwitchHack to anyone who owns a PalmPilot.

TealEcho!

On the CD-ROM

       Author: Vince Lee

       URL: http://www.tealpoint.com

       Version: 1.08

       Type: Shareware

       Cost: $11.95

TealEcho is a neat hack that displays Graffiti strokes as you draw them, in any application. Good for practicing (although I'd recommend Grafaid or Giraffe for serious practicing) or simply seeing how your strokes are turning out.

Figure 6.44 Example of TealEcho's output.

TealGlance

**On the
CD-ROM**

Author: Vince Lee

URL: http://www.tealpoint.com

Version: 1.10

Type: Shareware

Cost: $11.95

TealGlance pops up a little window each time you turn on your PalmPilot displaying things such as date, day of week, time, and upcoming ToDo and DateBook events. Many of these options are configurable, as is the ability to automatically turn on the backlighting when the PalmPilot is powered on (or during the 6:00 P.M. to 9:00 A.M. time frame). By issuing a double command stroke, you can also set up TealGlance to run only when you press one or a combination of the application buttons to power on the PalmPilot. I like setting Activate to the double command stroke option, as that makes TealGlance always available but doesn't display every time I power up.

Figure 6.45 TealGlance, showing upcoming events and to-do items.

TealMagnify!

Author: Vince Lee

URL: http://www.tealpoint.com

Version: 1.08

Type: Shareware

Cost: $11.95

TealMagnify allows you to show portions of the screen in a magnified window so that you can view items in enlarged type (for example, hard-to-read phone numbers).

Figure 6.46 TealMagnify's window showing an easy-to-read phone number.

Miscellaneous

Biorhythms

On the
CD-ROM

Author: Jeff Jetton
URL: http://www.mindspring.com/~jetton/pilot/index.html
Version: 1.5
Type: Shareware
Cost: $5.00

If you like charting biorhythms, this application is for you! Biorhythms allows you to enter birthdays for up to five different people, to easily track biorhythms for relatives and friends; or you can manually specify a single birthday and target date. You can also bring up a window that shows you, to the day, how old the targeted person is.

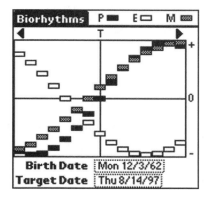

Figure 6.47 Tracking biorhythms.

Buzzword Generator

Author: Dave MacLeod

URL: http://www.netcomuk.co.uk/~davmac/pilot.htm

Version: 0.5

Type: Freeware

Cost: N/A

Do you need to baffle your clients, or just make yourself sound more intelligent? Try dropping "mandatory fault-tolerant knowledge base" or "right-sized homogeneous intranet" into a report or conversation and see what happens. This app will help you sound like every IT consultant you've ever met.

Country Codes

**On the
CD-ROM**

Author: Bozidar Benc
URL: http://www.flash.net/home/k/e/kenw/bbenc/
Version: 0.3
Type: Postcardware
Cost: Postcard

With Country Codes, you can find telephone access codes for most of the countries on Earth. Support for PalmPilot's Find function is included, so you can use the **Find** button to locate a specific country.

DigiPet

Author: Shuji Fukumoto
URL: http://www.wakuwaku.or.jp/shuji
Version: 0.9.5
Type: Freeware
Cost: N/A

DigiPet is a fun little application that closely resembles the popular Tamagotchi keychain sensation. Feed your DigiPet or it gets sick (and dies); chase it around for exercise or it gets fat. One recommendation: An option to turn off the alarm setting should be added because it can be embarrassing to have the little bugger wake up in the middle of an important meeting!

Digi-Guppie

> Author: Chris Henck
>
> URL: http://www.csam.montclair.edu/~hinck/guppie/
>
> Version: 0.5
>
> Type: Freeware
>
> Cost: N/A

Digi-Guppie does nothing more than display a little guppy or a little shark on the screen. You can also tap the fish, which will make it swim faster. This application was written in response to those who complained that the DigiPet application required too much attention to keep it going. Digi-Guppie can be ignored for weeks and will still be swimming strong!

EbonyIvory

**On the
CD-ROM**

> Author: Tony Leung
>
> URL: http://www.arcosoft.com
>
> Version: 1.0
>
> Type: Freeware
>
> Cost: N/A

EbonyIvory displays a little keyboard on the screen beneath an empty musical score. As you tap and play notes on the keyboard, the corresponding notes show up on the score, and the name of the note appears below the keyboard. I'd like to be able to see more than one note on the score at a time, and to record, save, and play back tunes after they have been entered/saved. Perhaps these features will be added in a later release.

Eightball

Author: Steven Wangner

URL: http://www.arkwin.com/flip/flip.html

Version: 1.5

Type: Freeware

Cost: N/A

Eightball is a computer simulation of the toy that you ask a question, flip over, and read the answer that floats in the window. Even the answers are the same.

Eliza

On the CD-ROM

Author: David Haupert

URL: http://www.gate.net/~dhaupert/ddhpilot.html

Version: 1.0

Type: Freeware

Cost: N/A

Eliza is the PalmPilot reincarnation of the psychologist game that many will remember from the early years of computing. The application starts by asking your name, and then asks, "Why don't you tell me what is troubling you?" As with the classic, Eliza proceeds to act (barely) on whatever questions or statements you give her.

FretBoard

Author: Dave MacLeod
URL: http://www.netcomuk.co.uk/~davmac/pilot.htm
Version: 0.6
Type: Freeware
Cost: N/A

A tool for guitar, bass, mandolin, or violin players, FretBoard displays notes, 25 different chords, and 16 scales, in every key. It also supports different tunings, and allows you to hear the selected note, chord, or scale.

Life

Author: Sean True
URL: http://striper.ne.highway1.com/pilot.html-ssi
Version: 1.0
Type: Freeware
Cost: N/A

The interesting game of Life has made its way to the PalmPilot. I have always been fascinated by this screensaver-like application, and the PalmPilot version contains enough features to make it just as intriguing. Place your spots on the screen, and start the game. Watch as mesmerizing patterns begin to form and disappear. Although probably not something you'll keep loaded on your PalmPilot for long, it certainly is interesting enough to install and toy with for an evening or six.

Moon

Author: Alex Garza

URL: http://200.4.12.1/~agarza/pilot/moon/

Version: 1.5

Type: Shareware

Cost: $5.00

This calendar shows you the moon phases for each day in any given month. Tapping on any of the days brings up a detailed window, with the current Julian date, the Moon's age (days, hours, and minutes) with percentage, and the number of days that have passed since January 1, 4712BC at noon.

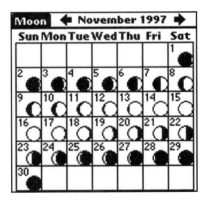

Figure 6.48 Moon shows you its phases.

Morse Code

**On the
CD-ROM**

Author: Eric Cheng
URL: http://www-cs-students.stanford.edu/~echeng/Pilot/pilot.html
Version: 1.0
Type: Freeware
Cost: N/A

Morse Code is a nifty little application that allows you to enter a string of text and then play its equivalent Morse code. You can specify the speed at which the Morse code is played, from slowest to fastest; the default is fast. If you are trying to learn Morse code, this just might be a handy application to have.

PilotEyes

**On the
CD-ROM**

Author: Ron Gouldner
URL: http://www.exit109.com/~ron/pilot
Version: 1.0
Type: Postcardware
Cost: Postcard

PilotEyes places a pair of eyes on the PalmPilot screen that follow the stylus as it moves. Though not what you'd call productive, this application is a great hit with kids and some adults as well.

Pilot's Wind Computer

**On the
CD-ROM**

Author: Bozidar Benc

URL: http://www.flash.net/home/k/e/kenw/bbenc/

Version: 0.5

Type: Shareware

Cost: $10.00

With this application, you can calculate headwind and crosswind, to ensure that the maximum crosswind component of an aircraft isn't exceeded.

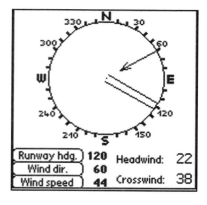

Figure 6.49 View cross- and headwind information with Pilot's Wind Computer.

pilOTP

On the CD-ROM

Author: John Valdes

URL: http://astro.uchicago.edu/home/web/valdes/pilot/pilOTP/

Version: 1.0

Type: Freeware

Cost: N/A

One-time passwords (OTP) provide a secure way to log in to systems over insecure networks. pilOTP allows you to generate an OTP without having to carry around a precomputed list.

PocketSynth

On the CD-ROM

Author: Eric Cheng

URL: http://www-cs-students.stanford.edu/~echeng/Pilot/pilot.html

Version: 1.23

Type: Shareware

Cost: $10.00

PocketSynth is a portable keyboard and music application for the PalmPilot. With it, you can compose and save songs on your PalmPilot (via cut and paste to and from the MemoPad application). Features include the ability to play back songs at various tempos, compose or play using a metronome tone, and an easy compose mode to enter complicated note series.

Figure 6.50 PocketSynth's Compose mode enables you to write a song on your PalmPilot.

PregCalc

On the CD-ROM

Author: Michael Hutchens

URL: http://davidge1.ab.umd.edu/"mike/pilot/pregcalc.html

Version: 1.21

Type: Shareware

Cost: $10.00

PregCalc calculates due date and gestational age, and can provide information about expected weight gain and lab results, and track appointments. You have the choice of entering last menstrual period (LMP) or expected delivery date (EDD), and the other will be calculated for you.

SiteSwap

On the
CD-ROM

Author: Stuart Macmillan

URL: http://www.geocities.com/SiliconValley/Bay/9526/
SiteSwap.html

Version: 0.09b

Type: Freeware

Cost: N/A

SiteSwap is a program in which you select and view different juggling patterns, called site swaps. Several options are provided, including specifying a random pattern or sound, and pausing an animation. SiteSwap is a handy tool for the PalmPilot-owning juggler, and it is a good demonstration of the PalmPilot's animation capabilities.

SoftGPS

On the
CD-ROM

Author: Brad Goodman

URL: http://www.oai.com/bkg/Pilot/

Version: 1

Type: Freeware

Cost: N/A

SoftGPS is touted as the first GPS application for the PalmPilot. When launched, SoftGPS shows you, in detail, your physical location by displaying a very large X and the words "You are here." Very funny stuff.

Tap Tester

**On the
CD-ROM**

Author: Jeff Jetton

URL: http://www.mindspring.com/~jetton/pilot/index.html

Version: 1

Type: Freeware

Cost: N/A

Tap Tester was written as a simple test program when the infamous Tap Bug was discovered in the new PalmOS 2.0. A subsequent system patch fixed that problem, but Tap Tester can still be used by new PalmPilot owners to determine before upgrading whether their machine has the bug.

Tricorder

**On the
CD-ROM**

Author: Jeff Jetton

URL: http://www.mindspring.com/~jetton/pilot/index.html

Version: 2.0

Type: Freeware

Cost: N/A

With Tricorder, you can scan for alien life forms or detect (or attempt to detect) intelligence in life on this planet. This fun application will provide you with hours of enjoyment. Try to find all of the hidden tricks in this app; and don't forget to press the page up/down buttons.

Figure 6.51 Scan for signs of stars with Tricorder 2.

Tuning Fork

**On the
CD-ROM**

Author: Tony Leung

URL: http://www.arcosoft.com

Version: 1.0

Type: Freeware

Cost: N/A

Tuning Fork generates a tone for the note A. Given this note, all other notes can be tuned by ear. The actual frequency of A is not cast in stone, however; it can vary from A338-A445, more or less. Therefore, Tuning Fork gives you the option to select a frequency in this range, as well as a length of time to play the sound.

Productivity

501 Scorekeeper

> Author: Steven Wangner
> URL: http://www.arkwin.com/flip/flip.html
> Version: 1.0
> Type: Shareware
> Cost: $5.00

501 Scorekeeper is for keeping track of two players' scores during a standard 501 dart game. Because you can enter the starting score, you can also use it for any similar dart game (1001, 301, etc.). After each player throws, enter his or her score and tap the **Subtract** button.

The alternative is the freeware application Sums, which lets you see each score as you enter it and allows more than two players. However, you must enter a minus sign for each score in Sums, whereas 501 Scorekeeper automatically subtracts.

Abroad!

**On the
CD-ROM**

Author: Yoshimitsu Kanai

URL: None Given

Version: 2.1

Type: Shareware

Cost: $10.00

Abroad! is a suite of applications to help folks who travel a lot. It includes a currency calculator, world clock, and unit conversion module. Abroad's World Clock module interface allows you to add your own list of cities and locate them on a mini-globe. Likewise, the currency and unit conversion modules are completely configurable, enabling you to make adjustments in both the current rate of exchange and to choose which currencies and units you want displayed. Although there are other applications available that perform these three functions, it's nice to have them all in one app.

Figure 6.52 Abroad's World Clock's city database screen.

AccessIt!

Author: Yamada Tatsushi

URL: http://www.tt.rim.or.jp/~tatsushi/indexe.html

Version: 1.0

Type: Freeware

Cost: N/A

AccessIt is a modified version of SimpleTerm by Iain Barclay. Sessions logs can be saved in MemoPad for later reference.

Agenda

**On the
CD-ROM**

Author: Matt Peterson

URL: http://www.dovcom.com

Version: 0.98b

Type: Shareware

Cost: $15.00

Agenda offers a view of your upcoming DateBook and ToDo entries in a compact, tabbed format. The four views available are: Today, Tomorrow, Week, and ToDo. For the Today and Tomorrow date tabs, you are shown the upcoming events, with the time associated with them (or a diamond for untimed events); for the Week tab, you are shown the date and time. ToDo items are shown only if they haven't been completed; they are also prioritized. In all of the screens, tapping on an entry takes you to the entry in the corresponding application.

Agenda is a handy application if you need to see an entire week's schedule (you can even set the default tab to a specific week). Note that Agenda is functionally identical to the commercial QuickAgenda application that ships with the QuickPac from Landware.

Figure 6.53 Agenda from Dovcom.

Analog Clock

Author: Mike Carlton

URL: http://www.isi.edu/~carlton/pilot

Version: 1.1

Type: Freeware

Cost: N/A

Analog Clock is simply that: a large, full-screen analog clock for your PalmPilot. Options included are to display the battery voltage and the current date.

AsciiChart

On the
CD-ROM

Author: John Valdes

URL: http://astro.uchicago.edu/home/web/valdes/pilot/AsciiChart/

Version: 1.0

Type: Freeware

Cost: N/A

AsciiChart gives you a view of the characters in each of the PalmPilot's built-in fonts, along with their ASCII codes. It also displays the height and width of any selected character.

AsciiChart can also be used to cut/paste characters to any other PalmPilot application. This is a handy alternative for those characters in the PalmOS fonts for which there is no Graffiti stroke or that do not display on the pop-up keyboard. Using AsciiChart, you can easily place these characters in any application that supports pasting.

Birthdate

**On the
CD-ROM**

Author: Wolfgang Fahl

URL: http://www.birthdate.com

Version: 1.1cd

Type: Shareware

Cost: $19.95

If you want to use your PalmPilot to keep track of birthdays, anniversaries, or other annual events, Birthdate is a program you'll want to register and use. To implement Birthdate, you simply put a person's birthday in his or her AddressBook record in a particular format. Or you can place more than one birthdate per AddressBook record, so that you can keep an entire family's birthdays in one place.

When you are done adding birthdates to the AddressBook, you are ready to run the application. Birthdate will scan the AddressBook records, pulling out birthdates, and then display them in chronological order. You can then select one to see the age of the person (or anniversary year); or you can have Birthdate insert a record in your DateBook for each birthdate it finds. You can even specify to be reminded to buy a gift/card a certain number of days in advance. Everyone who has ever forgotten a birthday or anniversary will appreciate the convenience that the Birthdate application affords. (Note that the version of Birthdate included on the companion CD-ROM has been set to expire in October of 1998.)

BugMe

On the CD-ROM

Author: Iain Barclay

URL: http://www.hausofmaus.com

Version: 2.3

Type: Shareware

Cost: $10.00

If you ever need to set an alarm quickly, BugMe was written for you. Using BugMe is simple: You scribble a note then select from one of the preset amounts of time, or choose **Custom**, and set a time and date for the alarm. This application is also useful when you need to time something, such as to boil eggs or to heat a baby's bottle. BugMe lets you set as many bugs as you like; each has its own page and graphics/scribble. I use BugMe for all those one-time alarm requirements, or for unscheduled periods (such as hour-long catnaps). BugMe is one of a handful of applications that I use on a regular basis, outside of the built-in PIM apps, and I highly recommend it.

Chronos

**On the
CD-ROM**

Author: Andrew Ball

URL: http://www.lon.hookup.net/~aball/

Version: 0.0.57

Type: Shareware

Cost: $7.00

Chronos is a clock/stopwatch/timer application. For months, the only Clock/timer/stopwatch application available was the commercial product Clock from Little Wing Software (which is great). Chronos is similar, but does not have alarms. Chronos does allow you to turn off the PalmPilot when you're using the stopwatch (or timer), something you can't do with Clock. All in all, this is a great application, especially for those not willing to spend $19.95 for Clock.

Figure 6.54 Chronos by Andrew Ball.

Commute

**On the
CD-ROM**

Author: Mike Koehler

URL: www.liii.com/~koehler/pilot.htm#http://www.liii.com/
~koehler/pilot.htm#

Version: 1.0

Type: Shareware

Cost: $10.00

Commute is a schedule manager for bus, plane, and train travel. You can enter departure dates and times, destinations and arrivals, and connecting schedules. After you enter the information into the application (by inputting data on the PalmPilot, although another method is due shortly), Commute determines the next departure time for a specific route and destination. If you've just missed a connection, the application can tell you when the next departure is. For anyone who travels extensively, Commute is a valuable tool.

Dictionary

**On the
CD-ROM**

Author: Scott Powell

URL: http://www.kagi.com/scottpowell

Version: 1.3

Type: Shareware

Cost: $20.00

This program is a translation dictionary, providing a fast and easy-to-use interface for looking up words in another language. You can select from a number of language modules: English/German, English/French, English/Spanish, English/Japanese. If you're a Win95 user, you can also create your own language modules using an accompanying program called MakeDict.

Doc

On the CD-ROM

Author: Rick Bram

URL: http://www.palmglyph.com

Version: 1.72

Type: Shareware

Cost: $12.00

Doc enables you to read very large documents on your PalmPilot. Written as a text reader, Doc has many features, such as bookmarks, automatic scrolling, find, jump to % or top/bottom, and selectable font view. Each document can be set to Private and selected for backup at the next HotSync.

To convert a text file to Doc format, you must use a MakeDoc utility, most of which are listed at **http://www.palmglyph.com/docutils.html**. There are also a number of useful Doc files located at **http://www. memoware.com**. Instructions on using Doc are provided (in Doc format) in the docinfo.zip file, also on the CD.

Doc is probably the application I use most often on my PalmPilot. I download my newsgroup and e-mail traffic into Doc to read when I'm away from my desk. I set bookmarks to any mail I intend to reply to, and frequently cut/paste sections out of various messages to use in my FAQ pages. Doc is essential to have on your PalmPilot.

By the time you read this, the latest incarnation of Doc, DocPlus, should be available. DocPlus promises the capability to edit files of any size. Most of the rest of its features are unchanged, with the exception of Find/Replace, Save As, New, and so on, which have been added to support the edit functionality. Be aware that DocPlus and Doc cannot run on the same machine, so if you think you will ever need to edit your Doc files, I recommend registering DocPlus.

Figure 6.55 Bookmarks are just one of Doc's many features.

EarthTime

**On the
CD-ROM**

Author: Scott Powell

URL: http://www.kagi.com/scottpowell

Version: 1.6

Type: Shareware

Cost: $10.00

This program displays a graphical map of the world and lets you tap on time zones to find out the various times around the world. You can also configure selected zones for Daylight Savings Time; the lower part of the screen lets you display three favorite cities and their respective times, which you select from a pre-built list of cities. EarthTime also shows IDD dialing codes.

Figure 6.56 EarthTime's map is easy to navigate.

FinFunctions

On the
CD-ROM

Author: Ben Cukier

URL: http://www.pipeline.com/~benjam/

Version: 2.02

Type: Shareware

Cost: $5.00

FinFunctions is a plug-in module for RPN, the popular calculator written by Russell Webb. FinFunctions adds two menus to the RPN menu list, and includes these functions: interest calculations, payment amounts, present and future value, number of periods/years, and payments per year. If you're comfortable with RPN and require access to these financial functions, look no further than FinFunctions.

FlyingPilot

**On the
CD-ROM**

Author: Bertrand Simon

URL: http://www.GpsPilot.com

Version: 1.01

Type: Shareware

Cost: $80.00

The FlyingPilot application works in conjunction with a GPS device (see GPS Tester, next, for more information on compatible devices and how to connect them to the PalmPilot). FlyingPilot gives you up-to-the-second information; the capability to create, edit, and otherwise manipulate your flight plans; instant reference to waypoint databases (available online); the option to define your own reference-points database; and more.

The GolfScore

Author: Eugene Tsai

URL: None Given

Version: 1.0

Type: Freeware

Cost: N/A

The GolfScore is a simple application for keeping a running golf score for a group of players. After you enter the initials for up to four players, the app displays a blank scorecard for the front nine. Entering scores is easy: Simply tap on the hole for each player and then select his or her score from a list of buttons at the bottom of the screen.

Though not as fancy as the offerings from Fighter Pilot Software (GolfTrac/GolfTrac Lite), The GolfScore does provide a good, simple scoresheet replacement. My only complaint? The available score buttons go only to seven, which is quite a bit lower than I tend to score on certain holes.

GPS Tester

On the CD-ROM

Author: Bertrand Simon

URL: http://www.GpsPilot.com

Version: 1.0

Type: Shareware

Cost: $20.00

GPS Tester is for testing your GPS setup with the PalmPilot, using the applications from Simon. The recommended GPS device is the DeLorme Tripmate GPS receiver, although two other brands (Garmin, Eagle-Explorer) have been successfully tested and used. If you don't see a GPS receiver listed, check the site to see whether one has been added. The cable required to connect the TripMate device to the PalmPilot is also available for purchase, at $20.00, plus $3.00 shipping and handling.

Hi Note

> Author: Bill Goodman
> URL: http://www.cyclos.com
> Version: 1.00
> Type: Shareware
> Cost: $15.00

The best way to describe Hi Note is to say it's a cross between an outline application and the MemoPad app. Hi Note enables you to create hierarchical memos, and move them around by dragging and dropping. Hi Note doesn't have some of the features of the Outliner application, but it is a good alternative for those who need a simple program of this type.

Hourz

> Author: Andrew Zaeske
> URL: http://www.best.com/~zaeske/zoskware.shtml
> Version: 1.1d
> Type: Shareware
> Cost: $20.00

Hourz is a time and expense tracking application for the PalmPilot. Using Hourz, you can easily track the time and money you spend on a specific project. You can then export this information in comma-delimited format to the MemoPad application, which makes that data available for exporting from the Desktop application to your favorite spreadsheet.

Image Viewer

**On the
CD-ROM**

Author: Art Dahm

URL: http://members.aol.com/PilotApps/

Version: 2.1

Type: Shareware

Cost: $17.95

Image Viewer is fast becoming one of the more popular graphics viewing programs for the PalmPilot. Image Viewer gives you the ability to convert, load, and view images from your desktop, in grayscale. The shareware version requires a short wait before you can view a picture, but this is absent in the registered version.

Image Viewer can contain as many images as you'd like; it helpfully displays a list of available images. Large images can be scrolled with the four application buttons. The program comes standard with a Windows application to convert .bmp files to a .pdb format, which can be installed on the PalmPilot using your preferred method. A significant collection of preconverted images is available for download from **http://www. memoware.com**.

JShopper

**On the
CD-ROM**

Author: John J. Lehett

URL: http://www.shoppersmart.com/jlehett/pilprogs.html

Version: 1.4a

Type: Shareware

Cost: $10.00

JShopper is a shopping list application. Some might argue that the ToDo list serves this same purpose, but JShopper is much more efficient, because you can build a database of items that you buy on a regular basis, from which you select the items you need to buy; a quick click on the **Need** toggle button displays only those items. Each item can also be linked to certain stores; and you can access a list of needed items for any store. You can also specify an item as a one-time purchase, and it will be deleted automatically after you have purchased it.

Figure 6.57 JShopper allows you to easily make a list of your staple purchases.

Kar Kare

Author: Lee Golden

URL: http://www.geocities.com/ResearchTriangle/6608

Version: 2.0

Type: Shareware

Cost: $10.00

Kar Kare is used to track mileage and maintenance statistics for up to four vehicles. You can enter your odometer and fuel readings at each fill-up, and keep track of your car's gas mileage. You can also enter maintenance events keyed to time or miles (three months or 3000 miles) and be reminded when it is time to perform that maintenance task.

MapView

On the CD-ROM

Author: Ian Goldberg

URL: http://www.isaac.cs.berkeley.edu/pilot/

Version: Null

Type: Freeware

Cost: N/A

MapView shows how to switch the PalmPilot into grayscale mode and move around an image that is larger than screen-size (drag your stylus on the image to see it work).

Outliner

On the
CD-ROM

Author: Florent Pillet

URL: http://w3.teaser.fr/~fpillet/pilot/

Version: 1.3a

Type: Shareware

Cost: $19.00

Outliner is actually two applications in one: It is an outline processor and a task management application. Creating an outline is simple: Tap on the **New** button and start writing. The **Add** button places another item in the same level, and menu and Graffiti commands add a demoted or promoted item. Moving items and tasks is also simple: Click on one of the four arrows in the top right of the screen to demote, promote, and move items. Once an outline has been constructed, you can export the contents, including numbering, to the MemoPad application. Outlines larger than 4 K will be split automatically by the export process.

Outliner's rudimentary task management lets you view a completion percentage and start/end dates. You can also go into a time line view, to see which tasks are currently active.

Figure 6.58 Example outline in Outliner.

Periodic Table

**On the
CD-ROM**

Author: Jerry Wang

URL: http://www.directlogic.com

Version: 1.00

Type: Shareware

Cost: $10.00

Periodic Table gives you access to a text version of the periodic table, which you can scroll to the various elements.

Periodic Table of the Elements

On the CD-ROM

> Author: Mitch Hoffman and John Gedroc
>
> URL: http://www.webcom.com/charla/chemlab/
>
> Version: 1.0
>
> Type: Freeware
>
> Cost: N/A

This is a Doc format listing of the periodic table of the elements. Elements are listed by atomic number, with symbol and atomic weight also listed. The Doc reader (or DocPlus) is required to view this file.

PhoneLog

On the CD-ROM

> Author: Shannon Pekary
>
> URL: http://www.handshigh.com
>
> Version: 1.05
>
> Type: Shareware
>
> Cost: $19.95

Using PhoneLog, you can keep track of the date, time, and length of all of your calls. This information can then be exported to the MemoPad database, and transferred into other applications on the desktop. To make data entry easier, PhoneLog will bring up a list of your AddressBook entries, from which you choose the party you're calling. You can also specify a description list ahead of time, which can then be selected from a pop-up list on the PhoneLog Edit screen.

Figure 6.59 Keep track of phone calls with PhoneLog.

Pilot StopWatch

On the
CD-ROM

Author: Chris DiPierro

URL: http://www.llamas.org/pstw/

Version: 1.10

Type: Shareware

Cost: $10.00

Pilot StopWatch runs up to five stopwatches at once. Capabilities include starting, stopping, pausing, and resetting each stopwatch, or performing any one of those options on all the watches at once. Certainly, there are other, perhaps more graphically pleasing, stopwatch applications available, but none provides five watches.

Figure 6.60 Pilot StopWatch gives you five stopwatches at once.

PostCalc

**On the
CD-ROM**

Author: Matt Peterson

URL: http://www.dovcom.com

Version: 0.5b

Type: Shareware

Cost: $10.00

PostCalc is simple application that calculates United States Postal Service (USPS) rates, including air and surface (when applicable).

ReDo

On the CD-ROM

Author: Rick Huebner

URL: http://www.probe.net/~rhuebner/redo.html

Version: 1.42

Type: Shareware

Cost: $10.00

Missing from the ToDo List application is the capability to specify repeating ToDo items. Enter ReDo. Using this application, you can specify items that ReDo will automatically insert into the ToDo List application according to rules you specify. You can have an item entered once a week or once a month, and you can specify the category and due date of the inserted item. ReDo will automatically launch and add any item at a specified time; and it can be set to launch the ToDo List after it has finished (so that when you wake up, the list will be displayed with the new items added).

ReDo also has an As Needed due date feature (set in Details for each item), which will place a checkbox next to that item. Selecting this checkbox will insert the item immediately into the ToDo List database, in the specified category. Used in conjunction with specific categories in the ToDo List, this feature gives you a simple generic checklist application (similar to ListMaker or JShopper).

Figure 6.61 Repeating ToDo entries is easy using ReDo.

Secret

Author: Andreas Linke

URL: http://www.tphys.uni-heidelberg.de/~linke/pilot/secret.html

Version: 1.5a

Type: Freeware

Cost: N/A

Secret is an application for storing more sensitive data in an encrypted format. You enter a number of up to eight digits, and then are presented with a screen to enter your data (which is automatically encrypted when you leave or tap the **Close** button). You can have up to five separate memos (called categories in Secret), and since the encryption/decryption process is automatic and based on the number you enter each time, you can have a different code for each of the memos (the others will appear garbled).

One problem with this application (and the other app like this, called Secrets) is that the page up/down buttons don't work like they should (pressing them scrolls only one line). A fix is promised in an upcoming release.

SmartShop

Author: Handyware

URL: http://w3.openlink.com.br/handyware/

Version: 1.1c

Type: Shareware

Cost: $12.99

SmartShop is a shopping list application. You define a list of shops and products to build a shopping list to take with you to the store. This list can include quantity, previous price you paid, and current price of the item. As you make each purchase, you can check it off of the list, then select **Total** from the menu to find the sum of all checked items.

SmartShop is a little more difficult to use than JShopper (described previously), but SmartShop does allow pricing, which JShopper doesn't.

Tax Calc

On the CD-ROM

Author: Frank MacBride

URL: http://www.macbride.com/pilot/~macbride/

Version: 1.0

Type: Freeware

Cost: N/A

Tax Calc is used to calculate the city and county transfer taxes in a real estate transaction. After entering those values, you input the purchase price and tap the **Calculate** button. Tax Calc requires the CASL runtime library to run.

TEAK

Author: Davis Programming

URL: http://www.davisprogramming.com/index_phq.htm

Version: 1.0

Type: Shareware

Cost: $44.95

TEAK, an acronym for Time, Expense, and Automobile Keeper, is an excellent application for tracking billable time, expenses, and automobile usage. The application allows you to track things at three levels (the defaults are client, project, and task), which are user-definable. TEAK makes accessing the other portions of the application a snap, via icons in all screens. If you need a convenient way to track expenses, take a look at TEAK.

TealMeal 2000

On the
CD-ROM

Author: Vince Lee

URL: http://www.tealpoint.com

Version: 1.01

Type: Shareware

Cost: $13.95

TealMeal is a restaurant database application you can use to select a restaurant based on certain criteria. Are you in the mood for Chinese or fast food, or do you want Chinese that is both cheap and fast? TealMeal, once data has been properly entered, helps you find just the right eatery.

TealMeal comes with applications that convert to and from TealMeal databases and text format, which means you can edit your data on both the Pilot and your desktop. Also provided (at **http://www.tealpoint.com/ software.htm#mealdb**) are prebuilt databases for select major cities.

Figure 6.62 Where do you want to eat?

Translator

**On the
CD-ROM**

Author: David Haupert

URL: http://www.gate.net/~dhaupert/ddhpilot.html

Version: 1.11

Type: Shareware

Cost: $12.00

Translator is a language translator program that can handle words, phrases, and compete sentences. Sixteen language modules are available for $12 each; the shareware version includes a demo version of the Spanish dictionary, which runs for 30 days. This application is a perfect companion for the frequent traveler who has to get by in an unfamiliar country.

Traveler

Author: Bill Ezell

URL: http://www.mv.com/users/wje/pilot.html

Version: 1.6

Type: Shareware

Cost: $10.00

Traveler is a currency and time converter. You can define up to three taxes, tips, or other percentage-based values, which are automatically applied when selected. The total is shown in the foreign currency and in your home currency. Results can be posted to a memo, and you can do reverse conversions. In addition, the exchange rate can be configured as either foreign/home or home/foreign. Last but not least, you can define an unlimited number of foreign locales and quickly switch to a different one (in the registered version).

Trip

On the
CD-ROM

Author: Shannon Pekary

URL: http://www.handshigh.com

Version: 1.3

Type: Shareware

Cost: $19.95

Trip saves you money by making it easy to track and categorize your automobile mileage for both business and nonprofit use. Subsequently, you can transfer these figures to IRS forms for painless tax deductions.

Trip automatically notes the final mileage, date, and time of the last trip for the car you are currently using. Then it computes the distance, and totals all the miles for a particular car and/or a particular category. Trip makes recording your miles so easy and fun that you won't ever forget to keep track of them again.

Figure 6.63 Entering travel details is a snap in Trip.

Tutor

On the
CD-ROM

Author: Scott Powell

URL: http://www.kagi.com/scottpowell/

Version: 1.0

Type: Shareware

Cost: $7.00

For anyone learning German, this program is a handy aid for practicing your vocabulary. It chooses words at random (in either English or German) and prompts you for the translation.

Words Per Minute

On the
CD-ROM

Author: David Haupert

URL: http://www.gate.net/~dhaupert/ddhpilot.html

Version: 0.96

Type: Freeware

Cost: N/A

Words Per Minute, or WPM, allows you to measure your Graffiti input speed. WPM comes with a test sentence, which can be changed. When you are finished entering the sentence, you tap the **Done** button and are shown a Results screen. This screen gives you statistics including number of words, number of errors, elapsed time, and words per minute. The program even keeps a list of the top 10 scores, so that you can see how well you (or your Piloteer friends) improve over time.

Programming

ASDK

Author: Darrin Massena

URL: http://www.massena.com/darrin/pilot/tanda.htm

Version: 1.0 Alpha 1

Type: Freeware

Cost: N/A

The ASDK, for Alternative Software Development Kit, is the collection of freeware tools compiled by Darrin Massena and others. If you are considering writing applications for the PalmPilot and don't want to spring for the commercial programming environment, ASDK is something you'll want to investigate.

cbasPad

Author: Ron Nicholson

URL: http://www.nicholson.com/rhn/pilot.html

Version: 0.81b

Type: Freeware

Cost: N/A

cbasPad is the BASIC programming language interpretation for the PalmPilot. Refer to Chapter 7, Programming the PalmPilot, for more information on cbasPad, including sample applications and a brief syntax list.

GCC Win32 for Pilot

Author: John J. Lehett and others

URL: http://www.shoppersmart.com/jlehett/gccwin32.html

Version: 0.4.0

Type: Freeware

Cost: N/A

GCC for Windows is the freeware C programming environment for the PalmPilot. Many developers are using this environment to write their applications, and although the learning curve is pretty steep, it's well worth the price.

Refer to Chapter 7, Programming the PalmPilot, for more information about GCC, including a sample program. And check out Andrew Howlett's excellent Tutorial (next entry) for more help with getting started using GCC.

GNU Pilot SDK Tutorial

Author: Andrew Howlett

URL: http://www.iosphere.net/~howlett/pilot/GNU_Pilot.html

Version: N/A

Type: Freeware

Cost: N/A

This is an excellent tutorial for the GCC programming environment. It defines a simple application with one form, one or two alert dialogs, one menu, and a number of buttons, fields, bitmaps, and labels. Although written with the programming newcomer in mind, it is also a good starting place for experienced programmers. And be sure to check out the excellent programming links and resources mentioned in Howlett's Web page.

PilotFORTH

**On the
CD-ROM**

Author: Neal Bridges
URL: http://www.interlog.com/~nbridges
Version: 0.4.0
Type: Freeware
Cost: N/A

PilotFORTH is an on-board FORTH compiler for the PalmPilot, intended to comply with the ANSI standard. Compilation speeds in FORTH are quite fast, comparable to those reached by C programs. Go to the PilotFORTH Web site for sample applications, and visit http://www.forth.org for more information on the FORTH programming language.

Utilities

AIR

Author: Peter Csurgay
URL: http://www.item.ntnu.no/csurgay/pilot/air/air.html
Version: 2.0
Type: Shareware
Cost: $5.00

AIR is an acronym for All In RPN, which means it provides applications such as WorldTime, Currency Exchange, Timers, Countdown Timers, MasterMind, and Music Piano, all in RPN, the calculator from Russell Webb (reviewed earlier in this chapter). You get the basic functionality of all these applications in a small footprint, and if you already have RPN registered, it's even better. Other applications are written to address these types of programs, but AIR is particularly great for those short on memory. Each registered copy of AIR is customized with your hometime and name.

AlarmHack

Author: Wes Cherry

URL: http://www.scumby.com/scumbysoft/pilot/

Version: 1.1

Type: Shareware

Cost: $5.00

A lot of PalmPilot owners complain that the alarm for the PalmPilot isn't loud enough. AlarmHack doesn't make the alarm any louder, but it does let you change several alarm characteristics, some of which can make it seem louder.

You can set the Alarm sound, and several aspects of how the alarm repeats. Another nice feature is the option to expand the confirmation of the alarm's OK button to cover the entire screen, so you don't have to poke around in the dark, trying to find the little button. Unfortunately, AlarmHack does not have a snooze feature.

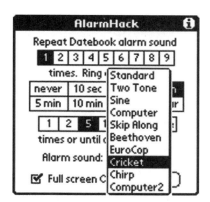

Figure 6.64 Various alarm options for AlarmHack.

Babel Encryption Utility

Author: Steven Wangner

URL: http://www.arkwin.com/flip/flip2.html

Version: 1.0

Type: Shareware

Cost: $15.00

This utility allows you to encrypt/decrypt anything that you have placed in the Clipboard. Babel then reinserts the encrypted/decrypted text in the Clipboard so that you can keep encrypted versions of your more sensitive data. Registered users who are also U.S. residents can obtain a 128-bit key version (the shareware version is limited to 24 bits). (For security programs that encrypt in place, check out Secret, SuperPad, and Pilot Secrets.)

Battery Meter

Author: Dave MacLeod

URL: http://www.netcomuk.co.uk/~davmac/pilot.htm

Version: 0.2

Type: Freeware

Cost: N/A

This very simple app displays the current (no pun intended) battery voltage, the level at which warnings start, the critical level at which the whole shebang shuts down, and the selected battery type.

Bmeter

Author: Matt Peterson

URL: http://www.dovcom.com

Version: 1.1

Type: Freeware

Cost: N/A

Bmeter is a simple application that shows the current battery voltage, instead of the bar in the standard applications picker.

Check-In

**On the
CD-ROM**

  Author: Jack Russell
  URL: http://dspace.dial.pipex.com/jakr/pilot/
  Version: 0.9
  Type: Shareware
  Cost: $10.00

Check-In's purpose is to display a time and information screen each and every time the PalmPilot is turned on, complete with clock and configurable user/owner information. You can also set Check-In to prompt for a password (set in Security App).

One of the more convenient features of Check-In is that you can display the Check-In screen always, or after a specified number of hours. This allows you to see the Check-In screen only first thing in the morning; for example, if you set the number of hours to, say, six, and normally turn on the PalmPilot more often during the day. Check-In requires the HackMaster extension PowerHack to operate, which is included in the .zip file.

Figure 6.65 Check-In's main screen.

ClipView

Author: Dave MacLeod

URL: http://www.netcom.net.uk/~davmac

Version: 0.1

Type: Freeware

Cost: N/A

ClipView displays the Clipboard contents, with a character and word count.

Explorer

On the CD-ROM

Author: Scott Powell

URL: http://www.kagi.com/scottpowell/

Version: 1.4

Type: Shareware

Cost: $20.00

This program presents data on your PalmPilot in a tree hierarchy, as in programs such as MS Windows Explorer. You can expand and collapse branches, view items (categories, to-do's, memos, etc.), create, delete, and move items. A new Folders database in the tree lets you create your own folders (and subfolders), and move and create the usual items (e.g., memos) inside the folders. The program also features a status bar with loadable applets, including a clock, battery indicator, and others.

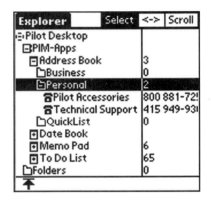

Figure 6.66 Explorer is a Win95-like interface for your PalmPilot.

Gamer's Die Roller

**On the
CD-ROM**

Author: Art Dahm

URL: http://members.aol.com/PilotApps/index.html

Version: 1.2

Type: Shareware

Cost: $7.00

This application is what every Dungeon master needs when playing Dungeons & Dragons. Gamer's Die Roller allows you to easily select a number of dice to roll and gives you the result; or you can choose a button to roll one die. If you play D&D and would like to use your PalmPilot instead of carrying that bag of dice, this application is for you.

Go Recorder

**On the
CD-ROM**

Author: Frans Velthuis

URL: http://www.rug.nl/~velthuis/gorec.html

Version: 1.0

Type: Shareware

Cost: $15.00

Go Recorder is an extensive implementation of an application that can record games of Go, to be played back at a later time. Also included is a PC application that can transfer the recorded games to the PC into SGF (Smart Go Format) files. Although I don't know that much about the game of Go, this application seems to have all the bases covered. It includes the entry of such things as handicap, ratings, game location, and Komi. For anyone who would like to record and later review a game of Go, this application fits the bill.

Grafaid

**On the
CD-ROM**

Author: Chris Crawford

URL: http://www.enteract.com/~crawford/grafaid.html

Version: 1.0

Type: Freeware

Cost: N/A

Grafaid is a slick little application that allows you to (hopefully) improve your Graffiti accuracy. Grafaid displays the Graffiti characters as you write them, as well as displaying the resulting text at the top of the screen. And, as an added bonus, you can also practice writing your characters on the screen. If you've been having problems with certain characters, Grafaid is a nice way to practice them and get instant feeback on what you might be doing wrong.

Figure 6.67 Grafaid shows Graffiti as you write it.

Graffiti Help

**On the
CD-ROM**

      Author: Bill Kirby

      URL: http://electronhut.com/pilot/

      Version: 1.6

Type: Freeware

Cost: N/A

Graffiti Help brings up a list of characters and their corresponding Graffiti strokes to remind you of those hard-to-remember strokes. Graffiti Help was released before PalmOS 2.0 (which has a built-in Graffiti Help screen that can be accessed from all the built-in applications) and I still prefer it, as its screens are more precise.

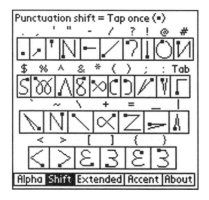

Figure 6.68 Learn those hard-to-remember strokes with Graffiti Help.

HackMaster

**On the
CD-ROM**

Author: Ed Keyes

URL: http://www.daggerware.com

Version: 0.9

Type: Shareware

Cost: $5.00

HackMaster is a system extension manager for the PalmPilot, for the purpose of patching PalmOS, to enable functions to be done/seen by any application on the PalmPilot. Although this can be done without going through HackMaster (programs such as Launchpad and QuickText do this), HackMaster performs some of the dirty work, and provides a consistent interface to install and uninstall these applications. HackMaster also makes it possible to reinstall all hacks after a soft reset (or not to, if you think one of the hacks might be causing the reset). Some of the more useful HackMaster extensions are FindHack, SwitchHack, SelectHack, and ClipHack.

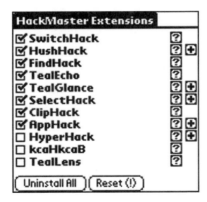

Figure 6.69 There are now a number of HackMaster applications available.

HTML Suite

Author: Harry Ohlsen

URL: http://wr.com.au/harryo/browser/

Version: 1.05

Type: Shareware

Cost: $20.00

HTML Suite is for converting and viewing HTML documents on your PalmPilot. Simply run an HTML document through the converter and install the resultant .pdb file. Then, using the supplied browser application on the PalmPilot, you can read and navigate through the Web page(s) while on the road. The converter application takes any linked local files and converts all of them to one install file. If you have a large site that is interconnected, you might consider moving some of the files before running the conversion application.

I use this for the browser version of my FAQ site. I simply make a DOS script that renames the files I don't want added to the browser file, converts the other files, and then renames the files to their proper names.

J-Info

On the CD-ROM

Author: Yoshimitsu Kanai

URL: http://www.sls.lcs.mit.edu/raylau/pilot/original/jinfo_ about.txt

Version: 1.7

Type: Freeware

Cost: N/A

J-Info provides some of the same base functions as the Abroad application (written by the same author) and adds Japanese-specific functions such as Japanese holiday list, postal price calculation, and age calculation. J-Info is written in Japanese, and requires J-OS written by Yamada Tatsushi (which is included in Yamada's Japanese Suite).

Launchpad

> Author: Eric Kenslow
>
> URL: http://www.nwlink.com/~emilyk/LaunchPad/
>
> Version: 1.11
>
> Type: Freeware
>
> Cost: N/A

When Launchpad first released, most PalmPilot owners were using the PAL application, arguably one of the most popular applications available. Launchpad changed all that when it introduced a tabbed interface that allowed the user to drag and drop applications from one tab to another. More significantly, Launchpad eliminated PAL's requirement to rescan the PalmPilot after installing each application in order for it to appear in PAL's list. And, perhaps even more important than auto-scan, Launchpad is freeware; PAL is shareware.

Launchpad makes it possible to add/delete/rename tabs, to automatically access tabs when the application's silkscreen button is pressed, and to set menu options to go to frequently used PalmPilot preferences and applications (I use the memory icon all the time). Launchpad is available in several different languages, including Spanish, Dutch, Hungarian, and French. (Note: Launch Em, part of the Hi-5 Suite from Synergy Solutions, is the same application as Launchpad.)

Figure 6.70 Launchpad's tabbed interface makes it easy to organize your applications.

LookAtMe

Author: Bill Ezell

URL: http://www.mv.com/users/wje/pilot.html

Version: 1.2

Type: Shareware

Cost: $10.00

LookAtMe is a combination alarm clock and application launcher. You can set a list of alarms to be repeated on assigned days. When an alarm sounds, the application associated with it is automatically launched, and the next alarm is scheduled. Alarms can be enabled or disabled individually or all at once. The duration of each alarm is also individually programmable; or you can use AlarmHack.

PaperClip

On the
CD-ROM

Author: Jeff Jetton

URL: http://www.mindspring.com/~jetton/index.html

Version: 1.0

Type: Freeware

Cost: N/A

PaperClip simulates inserting a paper clip into the back of your PalmPilot; in other words, PaperClip performs a soft reset.

Pilot Applications Launcher

On the
CD-ROM

Author: Matt Peterson

URL: http://www.dovcom.com

Version: 1.31

Type: Shareware

Cost: $12.00

Pilot Applications Launcher, PAL, is a replacement for the built-in applications picker. It allows you to define categories and place applications in them. In this way, you can organize your applications into logical groupings, rather than having one big list arranged in alphabetical order. PAL also lets you rename an application, so that you can effectively reorder applications within a category.

One downside to PAL is that you have to remember to rescan each time you add applications in order for them to show up. This wasn't a big issue when PAL was the only game in town, but Launchpad's automatic update now makes this seem like a chore. (Note: A modified version of PAL was renamed to QuickLaunch, and sells as a part of the QuickPac Suite from Landware.)

Figure 6.71 PAL lets you categorize your applications.

Pilot Secrets

Author: Al Bastien

URL: http://www.followme.com/abastien/

Version: 1.0

Type: Shareware

Cost: $12.00

Pilot Secrets is for storing your sensitive data in an encrypted format. Like the MemoPad application, you can have multiple notes, each encrypted with its own password. Encrypted notes are identified by a little lock icon.

PLoNK!

**On the
CD-ROM**

> Author: Brad Goodman
>
> URL: http://www.oai.com/Pilot/
>
> Version: 1.0b6
>
> Type: Shareware
>
> Cost: $5.00

PLoNK takes ToDo List items that are past due, and sets them as due today. You can set it to automatically "plonk" at midnight (by checking the **AutoPlonk** box), or you can run it manually.

Volume Control

**On the
CD-ROM**

> Author: Tan Kok Mun
>
> URL: http://home1.pacific.net.sg/~kokmun/pilotpgm.htm
>
> Version: 1
>
> Type: Freeware
>
> Cost: N/A

Volume Control enables you to control various aspects of the PalmPilot's alarm and system sounds. Three alarm levels can be adjusted: Alarm, System, and Master.

Figure 6.72 Change the default volume with this app.

WristRest

On the
CD-ROM

      Author: Iain Barclay

      URL: http://www.hausofmaus.com

      Version: 0.1d

      Type: Freeware

      Cost: N/A

WristRest is a simple utility to remind you to take a break from typing. Simply fire it up, select the amount of time you want to work before being reminded to take a break, and start typing (on your computer, not the PalmPilot). WristRest will sound an alarm when the time expires, and sound another one when break time is over. One limitation is that WristRest alarms will not work if you switch to another application. (Note: BugMe, by the same author, produces the same results but isn't limited to the active application.)

Conclusion

As I noted at the beginning of the chapter, there are too many shareware and freeware applications available for the PalmPilot to list, and anything put in print today is quickly out of date. The purpose here was to show you the depth and variety of applications you can choose from, and to direct you to other sources of applications, including current versions of those ones listed here. Enjoy!

CHAPTER 7

Programming the PalmPilot

In This Chapter

- Programming considerations
- BASIC and the PalmPilot
- Compact Application Solution Language (CASL)
- PILA
- GCC Programming Environment
- Commercial Compiler: Metrowerks
- Other languages
- Sample application using GCC

The PalmPilot is a very versatile device. Not only can you use it for its intended purpose as an organizer and PDA, but you can also download applications to it off the Internet. This chapter introduces the various aspects of programming on and for the PalmPilot.

We begin by examining the basic programming environments, and follow through at the end by walking through the process of creating a new PalmPilot application. The chapter won't make you a PalmPilot programming wizard, but you'll gain the knowledge you need to get started. And for those of you who want to continue where this chapter leaves off, pointers direct you to more information.

ROADMAP

To learn where to find each of the mentioned programming environments, refer to Chapters 5 and 6, the commercial software and shareware chapters, which include a brief description and list the URL for each program/company.

BASIC

BASIC, the acronym for Beginners All-purpose Symbolic, Interpreted Code, is an easy-to-learn computer language created at Dartmouth College in the early '60s. Its popularity is such that it can be found in almost every computer created since then. The version of BASIC for the PalmPilot, cbasPad, was crafted by Ronald H. Nicholson, Jr. as an experiment in writing a small BASIC interpreter in portable C. Based on Chipmunk BASIC, cbasPad starts with a very simple set of core capabilities, extended with several PalmPilot-specific commands and functions.

There are four good reasons to write applications using cbasPad. First, as already mentioned, BASIC is a very easy language to learn. Second, you can take the entire programming "environment" along with you, on the PalmPilot. Three, it might take some time to figure out the various PalmPilot-specific functions (following sections offer help on these), but once you do, you can write some highly capable programs in cbasPad. And, finally, the price is right. It's free! So let's get started learning how to use cbasPad.

Using cbasPad

After installing cbasPad on the PalmPilot, simply start up the application. The initial display, shown in Figure 7.1, is a blank screen. After applications have been written (or loaded), the display will list the various BASIC programs and fragments currently stored on the PalmPilot with a number followed by the first line of the program or fragment.

Figure 7.1 Initial cbasPad screen.

To create a new program, select the **New** button. To edit an existing program, just select the line containing the program and select the **Edit** button. To execute a program, again select the line, but followed by the **Exec** button. The example shown in Figure 7.2, is a basic cbasPad program. The explanation proceeds as if you were creating a new program, but note that editing an existing program is very similar. This sample has several good ideas that should be included in every program (although this is not required). The first line is a comment (signified by the pound sign—#—as the first character) that should identify the program in a short, meaningful statement, as it is used in cbasPad's program list screen.

Figure 7.2 Example Hello World program in cbasPad.

Everything typed in cbasPad's Edit window is sent to the interpreter one line at a time. Anything without a line number is treated as a command and executed immediately. Items with a line number are treated as program statements and are stored for later execution.

In the second line of Figure 7.2, which reads "new," should be the first command in any cbasPad program. It ensures that any previous programs are completely cleared from the interpreter. The next three lines are program statements, and thus are given line numbers. Although it's recommended to enter the line numbers in order because it is easier to identify problems later, you could put line 30 before line 20 and the program would execute in the same manner (the interpreter reorders the lines before execution).

The last line in the buffer contains the run command, which causes cbasPad to execute any programs currently in the interpreter, executing them in sequential order and proceeding until an "end" is hit, there are no more lines, or the user hits the **Done** button.

PalmPilot Support

The cbasPad program is a fairly standard, small BASIC, with if-then branches, for-next loops, go-to statements for flow control, and gosub-return support for subroutines. It does, however, have some additional built-in features that support the PalmPilot, which are listed in Table 7.1.

Table 7.1: cbasPad Features for the PalmPilot

Command	Arguments	Description
Dprint ?	Strings	Both print to a special mini-dialog box
grline	x1,y1,x2,y2,mode	Mode can be:. 1. Draw a line. 2. Draw gray line. -1. Erase line. 4. Draw rectangle. 5. Draw gray rectangle. 7. Draw filled rectangle. -7. Erase rectangle.
sound	freq, dur, vol	Play a tone (at frequency Hz) for duration milliseconds, at the requested volume (0–64).
	freq, wpm, vol, m$, [farnsworth_wpm]	Do Morse code.
sersend	Address, len, baud	Sends out serial data; if the baud is –2, then it's a function and returns the amount of data.
op	"ds",a$,x,y	Draws a string at x,y.
	"ds",a$,n*1000+x,y	Draws a string at x,y in font *n* (note that some fonts lack many characters).
	"sety",y	Replaces line y with following print statement.
	"page",a$	Changes output page to a$.
	"page","",n	Changes to output page n.
	"page","",-1	Creates a new output page and changes to it.
	"dt",t$s	Changes fn 30 dialog title.
	"it",t$	Changes input dialog title.
	"mfind",x$,n	Finds MemoPad entry starting with x$, sets n to index; or –1 if it fails.
	"dbrd","memo",n,m	Reads MemoPad entry n into s$(0); m is offset into record; if –1, starts on next line of memo.

Table 7.1 Continued

Command	Arguments	Description
(op con't)	"dbrd","addr",n	Reads AddressBook entry n into s$; lines longer than 31 will be truncated.
	"dbwr!","memo",n,1	Adds a line to memo n, last parameter; if 1, adds a newline after.
	"dbwr!","addr",n	Sets s$(0) through s$(18) in AddressBook entry n
	"db",type,create,n	Returns the length of database type record n; if create' is 1, create a new record; fn 80 will return address of this record.
	"gnum",n	Returns the first number from page n.
	"get$",n	Returns a string from line n of the current page.
fn	16	Returns seconds timer.
	17	Returns tick timer (100 Hz).
	18	Returns memory address of clipboard text.
	19	Returns length of clipboard text.
	20	Returns scaled battery voltage.
	24	Returns decimal date.
	25	Returns decimal time.
	30	Displays nine-line dialog; returns button status (s(0),s$(2), and so on are prompt values; s$(1), s$(3), and so on are default and return values).
	33	Waits for one Grafitti character.
	34	Returns tick time of last pen down.
	38	Nonblocking form of fn 33.
	39	Returns last input or dialog button status.
	42	Temporarily clears middle of screen.
	80	Returns memory address of current DB record.

cbasPad's Limitations

The cbasPad program has a few rather quirky limitations. Strings, in particular, have the most restrictions, in comparison to other BASIC implementations. A program can only have 12 string variables; cbasPad also has a single-string array predimensioned at 31 (s$), which means no other string arrays are possible. Only the = comparison is allowed, and + is the only operator that can be used.

The floating point is limited as well. For instance, the ^ operator must be parenthesized; for example, x = (y ^ 2.0).

In spite of these restrictions, if you're looking for a good way to learn programming for the PalmPilot, take a look at cbasPad.

CASL

CASL, the abbreviation for Compact Application Solution Language, is a commercial language (a demo version is available, which limits the application size; see Figure 7.3) from Feras Information Technologies. CASL programs can be compiled to run on either Windows or the PalmPilot, writing to the same database which can be kept up to date with HotSync, just as the PalmPilot's built-in applications.

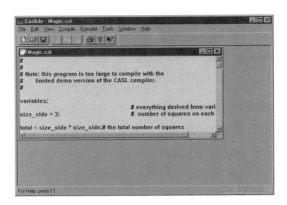

Figure 7.3 The CASL development environment window.

CASL takes a standard view of application construction for the PalmPilot. Basically, you describe the visual objects that your program will display, then provide code to be executed when those objects are triggered. You then test the program on Windows, download it to the PalmPilot, and execute it.

The CASL Interactive Development Environment (CASLide) contains tools for editing and compiling CASL source programs; testing them with Windows; and creating a .prc file, which can be installed on the PalmPilot. The compiled programs are actually p-code (a machine-independent language) that executes under control of the CASL runtime environment (CASLrt). This runtime module must be loaded into your PalmPilot in order to execute any CASL programs. Because it is needed by anyone who wants to run a CASL program, CASLrt can be freely distributed.

CASL is a good choice for programming the PalmPilot if speed is not paramount or you do not know C or C++. The price is competitive, around $69 at the time of this writing. There is a performance price to pay when running p-code, but most users do not notice it, as the applications spend most of their time waiting for input.

The following simple program produces the display in Figure 7.4.

```
variables;
    hello=1;
end;

frame helloWorld;
    display "Demo";
end;

label prompt, helloWorld;
    display "Hello World!";
end;

button press,helloWorld;
    display "Press Me";
    invokes pressMe;
end;

function pressMe;
    if hello=0;
        put prompt, "Hello World!";
    else;
        put prompt, "Goodbye World!";
    end_if;
    hello=1-hello;
end;
```

Figure 7.4 Output from the sample CASL application.

PILA

PILA is an assembler for the PalmPilot hand-held computer; that is, it takes 68000 assembler instructions and compiled resource files in one side and produces .prc files on the other. PILA is a Win32 console application (MS-DOS window) and runs under Windows NT or Windows 95.

Assembly language produces fast code that is usually smaller than comparable applications written in a compiled language. The disadvantages of assembly language are that it takes more time to write, it is more difficult to debug, and the source code to accomplish a task is generally significantly longer than that of a compiled program's code. The source code for a simple hello world application is included in the PILA documentation, so it is not included here.

PILA is the best choice for programs that require a lot of processing or are not overly complex. It is also appropriate for those situations where the programmer is fluent in assembly language (68000, specifically), or is willing to become fluent. It is not a good choice for anyone just starting out in programming or for someone who intends to produce a large and complicated piece of software.

GCC

GCC (GNU C-Compiler) is a publicly available, free C compiler for the PalmPilot, based on the GNU environment from the GNU Foundation. The particular version of GCC discussed here is for Win32, itself based heavily on another GCC for the PalmPilot that runs under the UNIX operating system. A Win32 console-based program, GCC closely resembles a UNIX programming environment, complete with makefiles, scripts, and so on. Best of all, GCC brings the power and speed of C programming to those who cannot afford the more expensive alternatives.

Installing GCC on your PC (carefully follow the install directions) will result in one of two setups, depending on which version of GCC you installed. If you are working with 0.4.0, you must go to a DOS shell to proceed. Version 0.5.0 enables a few shortcuts from the Start menu to speed you along. Note that because at the time of this writing version 0.4.0 was both the most widespread and the most stable version of GCC, the remainder of this section focuses on using it.

Before beginning, however, one caution: Anyone who is not familiar with DOS or who has never used a compiler in a UNIX environment probably should not attempt to program with GCC. GCC runs in a UNIX standard command-line environment called bash that can be a confusing environment for people whose experience with the command line stops at the default DOS shell prompt.

GCC, then, is for those familiar with DOS and/or a UNIX system, and on a tight budget. GCC works, it is fast, and it produces really good code for the PalmPilot. So if you are one of those people, you'll want to check out the sample GCC application given in the last section of this chapter. You may also want to check out the wonderful tutorial at **http://www.iosphere.net/~howlett/pilot/GNU_Pilot.html.**

Metrowerks

Metrowerks is the officially sanctioned development suite for the PalmPilot. It is the only package reviewed here that also has a version available for the

Mac, as well as Windows 95/NT. Metrowerks has a C compiler and a built-in IDE (integrated development environment). You can debug live on the PalmPilot, and Mac users have the option of using a PalmPilot emulator. Metrowerks also contains a GUI designer for building resource forms and the Conduit SDK for developing specialized applications for handling the HotSyncing of data.

This package is by far the most professional available. Its IDE and GUI constructor stand apart in their level of integration and usability. The downside is that, of course, you pay for this level of support. At the time of this writing, the compiler alone costs $369. If, however, you feel you need the level of support (and a lot of programmers do), the price should be no object. The power of the tools, the documentation, the integration, and ease of program design combine to make it well worth the price.

Other Languages in Development

The languages reviewed on the preceding pages are by no means the only ones available for writing PalmPilot applications; they are the ones mature enough to garner widespread acceptance and use. Two other languages fast approaching this level of maturity are:

- *Jump*. Enables PalmPilot programming in Sun's popular Java language. Jump takes a compiled Java application and converts it into assembly language (similar to a JIT compiler). That output is then fed into the PILA assembler to produce an application. A lot of steps, but it gets the job done.

- *BForth*. Very new at the time of writing, this is a port of the Forth language for PalmOS. This language has always been popular among programmers for dedicated devices (and at one time was the language used by Sun's boot PROMs). This would appear to be a language destined for the PalmPilot.

Still more and different languages and new versions of old languages keep appearing for the PalmPilot. This little hand-held device's capability to run third-party applications has engaged the imagination of the programming community. Where will it lead us next? That's for you to decide!

Complete Sample GCC Application

As a demonstration of programming a PalmPilot application, we'll break down a very simple game program, called Idiot Tic-Tac-Tie (or It-t-t). Everyone knows how to play tic-tac-toe. Players take turns writing Xs and Os in a 3x3 grid until either there are no moves left or one player has three in a row. Everyone soon learns that tic-tac-toe is a game that can always be forced to end in a draw. It-t-t is not that smart.

The basic algorithm used here, in simple English, is as follows:

1. Start a new game.
2. Ask the user if he or she wants to go first.
3. If yes, it's the user's turn; otherwise it's "our"—It-t-t's—turn.
4. If it's It-t-t's turn, pick a spot at random and set up for the user's turn.
5. If it's the user's turn, but It-t-t has won, tell the user and end the game (go to step 1).
6. Wait for the user to pick an unoccupied spot.
7. If the user has won, announce it, end the game, and go to step 1; otherwise, set up for It-t-t's turn.
8. Check whether there are any places left to move. If not, tell the user, end the game, and go to step 1; otherwise, go to step 4.

Now that the parameters of the game have been established, we can start writing the program. First, we need to create a resource file describing everything the user interacts with. This file is important because it contains the descriptions of all of the user interfaces that the program will have, and gives the application access to them. Resource files must be compiled (using pilrc) to produce files necessary to make the final .prc file.

In this game, only a few elements need to be put into the resource file: the menu, a dialog for deciding who will go first, PalmPilot and user victory dialogs, a draw dialog, the playing field, and finally, an icon that identifies and therefore initiates the program.

In an empty file (called It-t-t.rcp) we begin by laying out the menu, using the following lines:

```
MENU 1000
BEGIN
    PULLDOWN "File"
    BEGIN
        MENUITEM "New Game" 5000 "N"
    END
END
```

This fragment creates a single menu called "File," which contains the single entry "New Game." We could add more menus to the program simply by adding more pulldown-begin-end groups. Inside each pulldown are menu items (buttons for the current pulldown). These pulldowns are identified by an ID code (5000 in the example) and have a command key "/N." Additional items must have unique IDs and command keys.

Now it is time to design the necessary dialogs. We first add the following lines to the resource file:

```
ALERT 1000
HELPID 1000
CONFIRMATION
BEGIN
    TITLE "A question"
    MESSAGE "Do you want to go first?"
    BUTTONS "Yes" "No"
END

STRING 1000 "Answer yes to move first, No to move last"

ALERT 1001
HELPID 1001
INFORMATION
BEGIN
```

```
    TITLE "Congratulations!"
    MESSAGE "You've beaten me!  Try that again!"
    BUTTONS "OK"
END

STRING 1001 "Just press OK to go on"

ALERT 1002
HELPID 1001
INFORMATION
BEGIN
    TITLE "Yes!"
    MESSAGE "Victory is mine!  Hah!"
    BUTTONS "OK"
END

ALERT 1003
HELPID 1001
INFORMATION
BEGIN
    TITLE "A Draw"
    MESSAGE "No more moves left"
    BUTTONS "OK"
END
```

Notice the alerts used for simple message boxes and questions. Like menu items, alerts have IDs (in this case, 1000, 1001, 1002, and 1003). The HELPID associates a string (with the ID referred to by the HELPID) with the INFORMATION button on the message. Alerts posing a question are labeled CONFIRMATION, those displaying a message are labeled INFORMATION. Also available are WARNING and ERROR alerts, which are simply stronger forms of the INFORMATION alert.

Next we design the main form:

```
FORM 1000 2 2 156 156
USABLE
MODAL
HELPID 1002
MENUID 1000
BEGIN
```

```
      TITLE "Idiot Tic-Tac-Toe"
      LABEL "Written with GCC" 2000 CENTER 20
      GRAFFITISTATEINDICATOR  145 150
END

STRING 1002 "Time to play Tic-Tac-Toe!"

VERSION 1 "1.0.0"
```

This form is very simple, in keeping with the nature of the program. It is a labeled form, with a short piece of centered text. The rest of the application consists of drawing the tic-tac-toe board and moves.

The GRAFFITISTATEINDICATOR directs the PalmPilotOS to inform you what the pen is doing. It isn't necessary to this program, as it only shows how to use it. The coordinates indicate where to place it on the screen.

With the resource file written, it is time to add some code. The following is only one of many possible approaches for this particular application. Like the resource file, this has a simple start. We'll enter this code into a file called It-t-t.c.

A number of excellent alternative coding styles can be found on the Net. The RoadCoders site at **http://www.roadcoders.com/pilot/index.html** is a good place to look.

ROADMAP

```
/* It-t-t.c:  Simple test program
 *
 * (c) 1997 Chris Olson
 * This is free software, under the GNU public license v2
 */

#pragma pack(2)

#include <Common.h>
#include <System/SysAll.h>
#include <UI/UIAll.h>

#define MainForm   1000
```

```
Dword
PilotMain (Word cmd,
           Ptr cmdPBP,
           Word launchFlags)
{
    EventType e;
    Word who;
    short err;
    short i;
    short j;
    short move;
    short state = NotPlaying;

    if (!cmd) {
        FrmGotoForm(MainForm);

        for (; ; ) {
            EvtGetEvent(&e, 100);
            if (SysHandleEvent(&e))
                continue;
            if (MenuHandleEvent((void *)0, &e, &err))
                continue;

            switch (e.eType) {
            case frmLoadEvent:

FrmSetActiveForm(FrmInitForm(e.data.frmLoad.formID));
                break;

            case frmOpenEvent:
                FrmDrawForm(FrmGetActiveForm());
                break;

            case appStopEvent:
                return 0;
            default:
                FrmHandleEvent(FrmGetActiveForm(), &e);
            }
        }
    }
} /* PilotMain */
```

This code forms the skeleton of the application, and thus deserves some detailed explanation. The top part of the file is composed of a #pragma statement and three #include lines. These lines will appear in most PalmPilot applications. The #pragma statement tells the compiler that the structures are aligned on even-numbered addresses. (Version 0.5.0 of GCC does not need this line.) The #include lines ensure that the data structures and constants necessary for programming are available.

Next note the PilotMain function. This function is in every standard application; it marks the point at which every PalmPilot application launches. The first part of the program immediately checks whether the cmd is zero. If it is not, the application is not starting and is instead being told about a HotSync or other event. For most applications, it is recommended that the program do nothing but check for zero, because PalmPilots have been reported to act oddly, or even lock up, when even simple code is included before this check. One of the reasons for this is that global variables are available only on application starts. Alarms and HotSyncs (among others) do not make this area accessible.

After confirming that the application is running, we present the opening form (which we defined in It-t-t.rcp file above) and then wait for the PalmPilot to send events. Applications normally enter some sort of infinite loop to handle these events.

When an event is encountered, we need to let the system try and handle it first, unless we are really doing something interesting (or odd). The system may handle a pen-up event and transform it into a button event, which we are more interested in. After we let the system attempt to handle the event, we should determine whether it is a menu-related event, and let the system handle the menu if it is.

Thereafter, we must handle the event in some way. If the event does not interest us, we ignore it (the default case, previously). If we get an appStopEvent, we perform any clean-up and return 0.

In our program, if we receive a frmLoadEvent, we make the main form active (we can get fancy here, but we only have one form). Note the define used: It is always a good idea to use words instead of numbers if possible.

A frmOpenEvent signals that the form must be redrawn, so we do. Now the basic skeleton is in place. After compiling, installing, and running the application, the result will look like the screen in Figure 7.5.

Figure 7.5 Initial screen of the It-t-t application on the PalmPilot.

Not very interesting is it? We'll fix that by drawing the board. Remember, the frmOpenEvent is a clue that the application form must be redrawn, and that's a good place to draw the tic-tac-toe board. We'll add a function call, named drawBoard, after frmDrawForm call, as shown here:

```
case frmOpenEvent:
    FrmDrawForm(FrmGetActiveForm());
    drawBoard();
    break;
```

And to precede the PilotMain function, we'll add the drawBoard function itself:

```
static void
drawBoard (void)
{
    RectangleType r;

    r.topLeft.x = 30;
    r.topLeft.y = 30;
    r.extent.x = 100;
    r.extent.y = 100;
    WinEraseRectangle(&r, 0);
    WinDrawLine(63, 30, 63, 129);
    WinDrawLine(96, 30, 96, 129);
    WinDrawLine(30, 63, 129, 63);
    WinDrawLine(30, 96, 129, 96);
} /* drawBoard */
```

After compiling and executing this program, the result is the display shown in Figure 7.6.

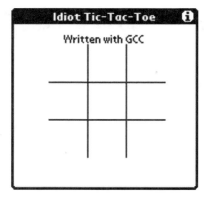

Figure 7.6 The It-t-t board.

Now it's starting to look like a game. One little adjustment is necessary, however: Because the drawBoard function will be called whenever the form is opened, we should update any Xs and Os on the board at the same time, in case the user switches to the application list and then back into the game, and the system is unable to save the display. To do that, we need two more functions (drawX and drawO), a global board to check, and a loop with which to draw the pieces. We'll add the following code prior to the drawBoard function:

```
static void
drawX (short x,
       short y)
{
    WinDrawLine(32 + x * 33, 32 + y * 33,
                32 + x * 33 + 29, 32 + y * 33 + 29);
    WinDrawLine(32 + x * 33 + 29, 32 + y * 33,
                32 + x * 33, 32 + y * 33 + 29);
} /* drawX */

static void
drawO (short x,
       short y)
{
    short tx;
    short ty;

    tx = 32 + x * 33;
    ty = 32 + y * 33;

    WinDrawLine(tx + 15, ty, tx + 24, ty + 6);
    WinDrawLine(tx + 24, ty + 6, tx + 29, ty + 15);
    WinDrawLine(tx + 29, ty + 15, tx + 24, ty + 24);
    WinDrawLine(tx + 24, ty + 24, tx + 15, ty + 29);
    WinDrawLine(tx + 15, ty + 29, tx + 6, ty + 24);
    WinDrawLine(tx + 6, ty + 24, tx, ty + 15);
    WinDrawLine(tx, ty + 15, tx + 6, ty + 6);
    WinDrawLine(tx + 6, ty + 6, tx + 15, ty);
} /* drawO */
```

Unfortunately, there is no draw circle function on the PalmPilot, so we pretty much have to fake it. We'll add the following code to call the drawing functions at the end of the drawBoard function:

```
for (i = 0; i < 2; i++)
    for (j = 0; j < 2; j++)
        switch (board[i][j]) {
        case 1: drawX(i, j); break;
        case 2: drawO(i, j); break;
        }
```

Don't forget, we have to declare the loop variables i and j at the top of the function:

```
short i;
short j;
```

Now we just have to declare the board to hold up the positions at the top of the file (right after the includes is a good spot):

```
static short board[3][3];
```

Note that we've declared the board (and every function except the PilotMain) static. This is a good programming habit to develop, especially for large, multiple-file projects.

Finally, we have enough pieces to start coding the game. Since the new game menu exists and is intended to start a new game, it's the logical place to begin coding, and so it is the first step in our design.

In PilotMain, right after the frmOpenEvent is handled, we add the following code:

```
case menuEvent:
    for (i = 0; i <  3; i++)
        for (j = 0; j < 3; j++)
            board[i][j] = 0;
    drawBoard();
    break;
```

In this segment, we do not check which menu is selected because this particular application has only a single menu. If we get a menu event, it has to be because the user wants a new game. If we had more than one menu, we would have to check the menu ID to determine which menu was pressed. The menu ID is in the event structure (e.menu.itemID).

At the top of the PilotMain function, we add the two loop variables:

```
short i;
short j;
```

This code clears the board of all moves, and draws the new board in case the user decides to play additional games.

Step 2 of our design is to ask the user if he or she wants to go first. Recall that the resource file contains an alert (ID 1000) that includes that question. It's a good idea to attach constants to these IDs for the sake of later clarity (as we did with the MainForm). We add the following lines after the MainForm #define:

```
#define WhoseFirst    1000
#define UserWon       1001
#define WeWon         1002
#define Adraw         1003
```

Then we add the question to PilotMain, right after the drawBoard function call in the menu event:

```
who = FrmAlert(WhoseFirst);
if (who)
    state = OurTurn;
else
    state = UsersTurn;
move = 0;
break;
```

The result of the alert determines who goes first, and we set the state variable accordingly. Notice that we need to keep track of how many moves have been made so we can tell whether the game has ended in a draw. Next it's important to define the states after the group of defines

```
#define NotPlaying      0
#define UsersTurn       1
#define OurTurn         2
```

and to add the state and move variables to PilotMain (right after the loop variables):

```
short state = NotPlaying;
short move = 0;
```

Since we just talked about it, now is a good time to handle the drawn game. Following the event switch, we'll add this code:

```
if ((state != NotPlaying) && (move == 9)) {
    FrmAlert(ADraw);
    state = NotPlaying;
}
```

This simple if-statement says that if nine moves have been made and there is no winner, then the game is a draw. We set the state back to NotPlaying and go on. We'll be checking the state variable to see whose turn it is, so this allows us to accept moves only from the user and pick our moves at the correct times.

In step 4 of the design, we decided that the next thing to do would be to pick our move. So we'll enter the following code between the event handler and the drawn game test:

```
if (state == OurTurn)
    if (win(1)) {
        FrmAlert(UserWon);
        state = NotPlaying;
    }
    else {
        do {
            i = SysRandom(0) % 3;
            j = SysRandom(0) % 3;
```

```
                        } while (board[i][j]);
                        board[i][j] = 2;
                        drawO(i, j);
                        move++;
                        state = UsersTurn;
                        if (win(2)) {
                            FrmAlert(WeWon);
                            state = NotPlaying;
                        }
                }
```

Notice that the first thing we do here is to make sure it's our turn; we do
not want to inadvertently move while waiting for the user to do so (a
possibility with event-driven programming on the PalmPilot). Next we
check to make sure the user has not just won the game. The function
determining this is placed above the PilotMain function:

```
static short
win (short who)
{
    short i;
    short score;

score = scoreBoard(who);
    for (i = 0; i < WINS; i++)
        if ((score & winTbl[i]) == winTbl[i])
            return 1;
    return 0;
} /* win */
```

This function is pretty strange, and the upcoming function scoreboard is
even stranger. But let's enter the scoreBoard function just above the win
function, then we'll discuss both:

```
static short
scoreBoard (short player)
{
    int i;
    int j;
    short score;
```

```
    score = 0;
        for (i = 0; i < 3; i++)
            for (j = 0; j < 3; j++)
                if (board[i][j] == player)
                    score |= 1 << ((i * 3) + j);
        return score;
    } /* scoreBoard */
```

Those two functions were written to make determining whether the game is over easier to code. It relies on C's ability to manipulate bits to easily set up what otherwise would be eight really complicated if-statements. Scoreboard simply encodes the board as a 9-bit number (with each bit corresponding to a position on the board). Win then compares the bits set in the score with a short table of winning scores. If it finds a match, 1 is returned; otherwise, 0 is returned. The winning board positions need to be entered somewhere above the score (just after the other defines at the top of the file is recommended):

```
/*
 *   0   1   2
 *
 *   3   4   5
 *
 *   6   7   8
 */
#define B(x) (1<<(x))

static short winTbl[] = {
    B(0)|B(1)|B(2), B(0)|B(4)|B(8), B(0)|B(3)|B(6),
    B(1)|B(4)|B(7), B(2)|B(4)|B(6), B(2)|B(5)|B(8),
    B(3)|B(4)|B(5), B(6)|B(7)|B(8),
};
#define WINS    8
```

Now, back to how the PalmPilot will pick its move. It's really simple (idiotic really, hence the name of our application). It picks a square at random until it finds one that is unoccupied, occupies it, checks to see if it has won, increments the move, and goes on.

The only thing left to do is get the player's move. That, too, is simple. We add the following code after the menu event in the event-handling switch:

```
case penUpEvent:
    i = (e.screenX - 30) / 33;
    j = (e.screenY - 30) / 33;
    if (i >= 0 && i <= 2 && j >= 0 && j <= 2 &&
        !board[i][j] && state == UsersTurn) {
        board[i][j] = 1;
        drawX(i, j);
        state = OurTurn;
        move++;
    }
    break;
```

This code waits for a pen-up event, figures out which square the user picked, determines whether the square is available, and if it is the user's turn. If so, it marks it, draws it, and increments the move. The program is complete. When executed and a few moves are played, we have the result in Figure 7.7.

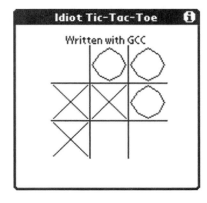

Figure 7.7 Finally, we're done!

This program is a good example of how to program the PalmPilot, but it's far from perfect. In particular, the PalmPilot does not make very smart moves, and the interface could use a little sprucing up. These improvements are good practice tasks. The source code for the complete program, as well as the makefile to build it, are included on the CD. Use what is shown here as a jumping-off point to many enjoyable and useful programs for the PalmPilot.

ROADMAP

There are two good online resources for new and experienced PalmPilot programmers. The first is RoadCoders, which provides articles about programming the PalmPilot, and pointers to other programming Web sites. Find RoadCoders at **http://www.roadcoders.com**. The other site is Wade's Pilot Programming FAQ, which answers frequently asked questions about programming the PalmPilot. Wade's FAQ can be found at **http://www.wademan.com/Pilot/Program/FAQ.htm**.

Conclusion

Now that we've looked at the basic elements of programming the PalmPilot and talked about a couple of programming online resources, let's look at some other online resources for the PalmPilot in the next chapter.

CHAPTER 8

PalmPilot Online Resources

In This Chapter

- Calvin's PalmPilot FAQ
- Other FAQs
- PalmPilot mailing list
- PalmPilot-related USENET newsgroups
- America Online and CompuServe support
- Internet relay chat (IRC) and the PalmPilot
- Online software archives
- Other online resources

There are literally hundreds of Web pages dedicated to the PalmPilot, with more being added daily, so it is impossible to list and review here all of the online resources available to the PalmPilot owner. Therefore, this chapter highlights the more informative places to go online to find information and software about the PalmPilot.

Calvin's PalmPilot FAQ

As I explained at the beginning of this book, my PalmPilot FAQ site is the foundation on which *The Complete PalmPilot Guide* is based. Launched in January 1997, this site quickly grew into a primary source of information on the PalmPilot (see Figure 8.1). Initially intended to answer frequently asked questions, it soon became apparent that it could and should serve other purposes, so today Calvin's PalmPilot FAQ consists of these six main areas:

- *Frequently Asked Questions (**http://www.pilotfaq.com**)*. Sixty-plus questions and answers about the PalmPilot that aren't covered in the documentation. Also offers hints to make using the PalmPilot a little easier.

- *IRC/AOL chat information and logs (**http://www.pilotfaq.com/ chatlogs.htm**)*. Information on the biweekly PalmPilot online informal chat sessions and the monthly America Online sessions.

- *Links to all PalmPilot-related Web sites (**http://www.pilotfaq.com/ links.htm**)*. A comprehensive list of all known PalmPilot-related Web sites, broken down into these four areas: Software, News and Information, Programming, and Commercial.

- *Calvin's PalmPilot Reviews (**http://www.pilotfaq.com/ reviews.htm**)*. Reviews and accompanying screenshots from selected PalmPilot applications.

- *Calvin's PalmPilot FAQ Site of the Week (**http://www.pilotfaq.com/siteweek.htm**).* Highlights a Web site that deserves special attention. Includes a list of past winners.

- *What's on Calvin's PalmPilot? (**http://www.pilotfaq.com/mypilot.htm**).* A list of the software that is currently installed on my PalmPilot, for the insanely curious.

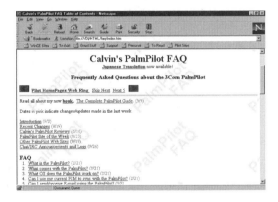

Figure 8.1 The main page of Calvin's PalmPilot FAQ Website.

Calvin's PalmPilot FAQ online address is ***http://www.pilotfaq.com***. The entire site has also been reproduced on this book's companion CD-ROM. See Appendix A, What's on the CD, for the site's location on the disc.

ROADMAP

The questions, answers, and other information on Calvin's PalmPilot FAQ changes frequently. Therefore, the CD-ROM copy of the site should be regarded only as a jumping-off point. For the most current information, go to the online site.

NOTE

Other FAQs

There are several other online FAQ pages dedicated to PalmPilot information. Each of these sites has its own advantages: one may be smaller and therefore easier to navigate; another may offer a different slant on a question. There are always various ways to approach problems, so search all the sites to find the solution that most appropriately solves yours.

- The first PalmPilot FAQ in HTML format, written by Neil Weisenfeld (**http://www-etb.info.nih.gov/~weisen/pilot_faq.html**). Started in late November 1996, this site isn't updated on a regular basis.

- Ron Nicholson's "quick and dirty" text-only PalmPilot FAQ (**http://www.nicholson.com/rhn/pilot.html**). This condensed FAQ covers the most important and most asked questions concerning the PalmPilot.

- Holger Klawitter's German Pilot FAQ site (**http://wwwmath.uni-muenster.de/~holger/pilot/faq.html**).

- 3Com's Frequently Asked Questions (**http://www.3com.com/palm/custsupp/faq.html**). This FAQ site focuses only on the basic aspects of the PalmPilot, such as PalmOS 2.0 and the NetSync product.

The PalmPilot Mailing List

The PalmPilot mailing list is a high-traffic list, so you should expect to receive between 20 and 50 messages a day. If this level of information on a daily basis proves too overwhelming, and therefore unproductive, you can choose to receive the list in digest form, in which case you'll receive just one compiled message every day. Another low-traffic alternative is the announcement-only PalmPilot mailing list, which is moderated and sends out only important software announcements, news from 3Com, and other newsworthy items.

Here's how to access these three mailing lists:

- *The original multiple-message list.* Send an e-mail message to pilot-request@freeside.ultraviolet.org. Use the word **subscribe** in the body of the message. (Note that because of the high volume of traffic at this site, it is requested that anyone posting to the list follow standard Internet mailing list netiquette. If you need information on what is essentially Internet etiquette, and how specifically it relates to mailing lists, go to **http://rs6000.adm.fau.edu/rinaldi/net/dis.html.**)

- *The digest version.* Send an e-mail message to pilot-digest-request@freeside.ultraviolet.org. Use the word **subscribe** in the body of the message.

- *The announcement-only version.* Send an e-mail message to pilot-announce-request@freeside.ultraviolet.org. Again, include the word **subscribe** in the body of the message.

To unsubscribe to any of these lists, send an e-mail message to the same addresses listed above, but instead of typing subscribe, use **unsubscribe**. If you have any problems unsubscribing, check one of the headers of the messages you have been receiving to confirm that you are using the correct address. Remember, you must reproduce the address *exactly* or your request cannot be fulfilled.

PalmPilot-Related Newsgroups

PalmPilot-related information can also be had from a number of Internet newsgroups. Try one of these:

- alt.comp.sys.palmtops.pilot
- comp.sys.handhelds
- comp.sys.palmtops
- comp.sys.palmtops.pilot
- comp.sys.pen

The first, alt.comp.sys.palmtops.pilot, contains the most information that relates directly to the PalmPilot. However, because it is an alt newsgroup and not one of the "big 8," not all newsgroup servers will carry it, especially those associated with businesses.

Online Services

Two of the popular online services provide areas to discuss the PalmPilot. These areas provide an informal setting to receive answers and support from your fellow PalmPilot owners, as well as software to download, general information, and online chat sessions.

CompuServe

The CompuServe Palmtop B Forum has a section for discussions about the PalmPilot that is extremely active and informative. It is often monitored by the folks at Palm Computing.

America Online

On AOL, Palm Computing maintains a support area for users at Keyword PALM, and various PalmPilot resources can be tapped at keyword PDA. And, on the second Tuesday of each month, a PalmPilot chat night is hosted on the discussion forum.

Internet Relay Chat IRC Sessions

On DALnet, one of the many available IRC networks, channel #pilot-pda, an informal meeting for PalmPilot owners and developers takes place every Wednesday and Sunday night at 8:30 Central Standard Time. During these discussions, which range from scheduled talks, complete with featured guests, to unformatted free-for-alls, everyone shares their thoughts about the current PalmPilot applications or trends.

For more information on DALnet, go to **http://www.dalnet.com**. If you need an IRC client, try mIRC for the PC, and Ircle or Homer for the Mac. You can get these and other IRC clients directly from the DALnet FTP site (**ftp://ftp.DAL.net/dalnet/clients/**).

Software Archives for the PalmPilot

A number of sites have links to the various applications that are available for the PalmPilot, but here are three that stand out from the rest.

Stingersoft

One of the original PalmPilot sites, Stingersoft sets itself apart by enabling developers (anyone, actually) to add content to it, including new PalmPilot software, a new PalmPilot Web page links (see Figure 8.2), or news. No wonder, then, that Stingersoft is one of the most popular PalmPilot sites on the Internet. In addition to its up-to-date database, it offers a mailing list you can join, which will automatically notify you of any updates to the site. To get Stingersoft, point your Web browser to **http://pilot. cc-inc.com/stinger/stingersoft.cfm**.

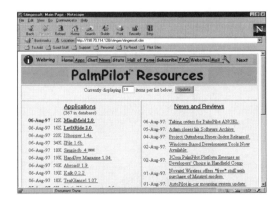

Figure 8.2 The Stingersoft main page.

PalmPilotGear HQ

A more recent arrival, PalmPilotGear HQ proclaimed that it would become the one and only site to visit for PalmPilot-related information, software, and accessories—a promise hard to live up to. Still, PalmPilotGear has made inroads to accomplishing this goal. Listing more applications than Stingersoft, PalmPilotGear HQ allows direct registration of certain shareware applications, and sells most available accessories for the PalmPilot. The site also allows direct updating of its application database, which, as a result, is remarkably current. Each application contains a description, Web page author's e-mail address (if applicable), and much more (see Figure 8.3). Visit PalmPilotGear HQ at **http://www. pilotgear.com**.

Figure 8.3 A typical application page at PalmPilotGear HQ.

See the PalmPilotGear HQ coupon at the back of this book for a savings on any purchase from the company.

ROADMAP

Ray's USR PalmPilot Software Archive

On another manually updated site, Ray keeps track of new PalmPilot-relevant releases, including a description, author e-mail, and a "local copy" of each application, which ensures that if the original site is down, you will still be able to download the latest in PalmPilot software from Ray's site. Find Ray's PalmPilot software archive at **http://www.palmpilotfiles.com**.

Web Links

Although it is impossible to keep track of the hundreds of PalmPilot-related Web sites, I do manage to maintain a comprehensive list. Located at my Web site (and on the book's companion CD-ROM), the list is broken into five categories:

- New or recently discovered links: **http://www.pilotfaq.com/links.htm**

- Links to PalmPilot software sites—sites that support a specific application or applications: **http://www.pilotfaq.com/linksoft.htm**

- Links to news and information sites: **http://www.pilotfaq.com/linknews.htm**

- Links to programming-related sites: **http://www.pilotfaq.com/linkprog.htm**

- Links to commercial sites: **http://www.pilotfaq.com/linkcomm.htm**.

Conclusion

New online sites dedicated to the PalmPilot spring up every day. While I've attempted to cover the more popular sites, this list could change, as popular sites close and new sites grow in popularity. In addition, what I feel are popular sites may not be considered so by other PalmPilot owners. Because of this, I highly recommend that you start with the sites I've mentioned and explore the ever-evolving online PalmPilot community, and find *your* favorites.

Appendix A

What's on the CD

The CD-ROM contains an index.htm file that links to all the other directories/folders on the CD-ROM.

These directories, and their contents, are as follows:

FAQs

The complete contents of my FAQ site, on disc. (Located in the \faq Win 95 directory and the **faq** folder for Mac users.)

SDK Documentation

The PalmOS 1.0 and 2.0 Software Development Kit documentation, in Adobe Acrobat format. This documentation has been downloaded directly from the 3Com/Palm Computing Web site. Adobe Acrobat Reader is needed to view this text. Acrobat Reader can be downloaded at the Adobe site at **http://www.adobe.com**. (Located in the **\sdkdocs** Win 95 directory and in the **sdkdocs** folder for Mac users.)

Software

Shareware/freeware and commercial demos for the PalmPilot. Each application is contained in its own directory/folder, and most include installation instructions and documentation. Each application on the CD is also described in the book. Applications that appear on the CD are denoted in those chapters with an "on the CD" icon. (Located in the **\software** Win 95 directory and in the **Software** folder for Mac users.

The CD-ROM is a dual format, for Windows 95 and Macintosh users. Following is a list of files (folders) for each version.

\software\win95\Commercial

AtheleteCalc

CASL

ListMaker

Palmeta Mail

readme.txt

SynCalc

SynCalcPP

WorldTime

\software\win95\Shareware

4inLine

AAGradient

Abacus

Abroad

AGB

Agenda

AlCalc

AppHack

ASCIIChart

Ataxx

BackHack

BasicGamePack

BasicUtilityPack

BinCalc

Biorhythms

BirthDate

BlackBox

BlackJack

Blackout

Blocks

Boxes

BugMe

Check-In

Chronos

ClipHack

Commute

CountryCodes

CurrCalc

Dictionary

DinkyPad

Doc

Dots

DrugDosage

EarthTime

EbonyIvory

Eliza

EmeraldHunt

Explorer

FeNaCalc

FinFunctions

FlipIt

FlyingPilot

Fore

FreeCell

GamersDieRoller

GemHunt

GolfSolitaire

GoRecorder

GPSTester

Grafaid

GraffitiHelp

GuessMe

HackMaster

Hangman

Hit

HMaki

HushHack

ImageViewer

inComing

J-Info

JFile

Jookerie

JShopper

JTWOF

Kalk

Klondike

LetItRide

LoanCalc

MakeDocW

MapView

MathPad

MED

MenuHack

MindMeld

MissileCmd

MoneyCalc

MorseCode

MusicBox

Outliner

PAL

PalmDraw

Palmscape

Paperclip

Pegged

PeriodicTable

PeriodicTable4Doc

Perplex

PharmacyCalc

PhoneLog

Pikoban

PilotADR

PilotEyes

PilotFORTH

PilotOTP

PilotPal

PilotStopwatch

PilotsWindComputer

PInstall

Plonk

PocketSynth

Pong

PostCalc

PregCalc

Pyramid

Q-Mate

Rally1000

readme.txt

ReDo

SelectHack

SimpleDB

SingleNumber

SiteSwap

SketchPad

Slots

SoftGPS

Sokoban

SwitchHack

TapTester

TaxCalc

TealEcho

TealGlance

TealMagnify

TealMeal2000

TealPaint

TedTruss

TicTacToe

TopGunPostman

TopGunTelnet

Translate

Tricorder

Trip

TuningFork

Tutor

VolumeControl

WheelofTreasure

WordsPerMinute

WristRest

yahtc

zip

\software\mac\Commercial

The Macintosh commercial application folder is identical to the Windows 95 directory.

\software\mac\Shareware

The Macintosh shareware application folder is identical to the Windows 95 directory, with the following Macintosh-only files added:

FixPDBDates

CoPilot

Web2Pilot

Also, the following Windows 95 applications are not available for the Mac:

MakeDocW

PilotADR

PilotPal

PInstall

Index

Index

....

PalmPilotGear H.Q. is the one-stop resource for all PalmPilot hardware, software, and accessories. We carry a full line of accessories for the PalmPilot, including custom cases, styli, screen protectors and enhancements, and many other products that will make your PalmPilot easier to use. We also maintain the most comprehensive database of PalmPilot software applications in the world, including commercial software and shareware.

Visit PalmPilotGear H.Q. at http://www.palmpilotgear.com or contact us at:

(800) 741-9070
(817) 461-3480
(817) 461-3482 FAX
sales@palmpilotgear.com

Fill out this coupon and return it to us at the address below and receive $5.00 off your first phone order. (Limit one item per household.)

Name _____ Email _____

Address _____

City _____ State _____ Zip _____

Phone _____

Would you like a catalog? Yes _____ No _____

Would you like to be notified of new products and software by e-mail?

Yes _____ No _____

Send to: PalmPilotGear H.Q., 1521 N. Cooper, Suite 790, Arlington, TX 76011